SEX AND ALLAH

CHRISTIAN PRINCE

VOLUME I

DEDICATION

Once upon a time a King ordered his Tailor to make for him such an exceptional clothing like no one had ever seen before, and that if he wouldn't like it, he is going to execute the Tailor.

And the Tailor was so smart, therefore he told the king he is going to make a special clothing for him which only can be seen by those who are trustworthy and loyal to him, and which the foolish and the liars, and anyone that hates him can't see!

The day to wear those magical clothes came, and the Tailor acted as if he was dressing the king up. Although the king noticed that he wasn't wearing any clothing yet, he was afraid to say: I don't see those clothes on me. After all the Tailor previously told him: fools and liars cannot see it!

The king walked in the festival totally naked and all of the crowd was so shocked, but none of the crowd there dared to say: the king is naked! Otherwise he would be accused to be foolish and to hate the king!

But a child of God by the name of Christian prince, he did say loud and clear: the King is naked!!!

For That Was The Truth

I hope you will enjoy reading my book about the naked truth which nobody dares to say.

TABLE OF CONTENTS

NOTICE

Seks & Allah, volume I.

You are about to read volume one of two volumes.

Together *Sex & Allah volume I & II* cover the extensive subject of sexuality and Islam. For your convenience I decided to divide *Sex & Allah* into two practical volumes. Volume two continues where volume one ends.

This first volume starts off giving you unique knowledge about pre-Islamic sexual practices and regulations, and will gradually narrow down to the founder and role model of Islam, Mohammed, showing in great detail his influence in the development, formation and implementation of sexual rules and regulations in Islam.

May I recommend you, after finishing this first volume to continue exploring the incredible Islamic logic regarding sexuality. The second volume continues with sex in Muhammad's universe, his special privileges, takes you through the intriguing Islamic interspace between human and non human: sexual activities of jinns, Satan, angels, and will finally leave you with prospects of infinite sex within the realms of the Islamic hereafter.

Please take a note that any translation that is not showing the name of the translator next to the Quran verse or Hadith, for sure is a Christian Prince translation.

INTRODUCTION

Imam Al-'Hafiz, and Ibn 'hajar in the book of Fat'eh Al-bari. Said: " anyone he fear Allah, Allah would make him extremely horny, and this is was one of the privilege of the prophet, may Allah pray on him and salute him, therefore he used to do intercourse for all his Women everyday" volume 1, page 282

وقال الحافظ (3) ابن حجر في «فتح الباري»: قالوا: كل من كان أتقى لله كان أشد شهوة، واعلم أن هذه الخاصية له صلى الله عليه وسلم قد ظهر أثرها في أنه صلى الله عليه وسلم كان يطوف على نسائه في اليوم الواحد

The wise Al Turmizi said: the prophets Allah increased their ability to do intercourse because of the blessing of being lighted (with knowledge and belief), because of the chest is full with it, is going to flood the nerves and the pleasure would be overwhelming traveling through the nerves and inquiry is the sexual desire" Al-Tanwir fi Sharih Al-jami' Al-'Saqir volume 1. Page 282

قال الحكيم (٤) الترمذي في «نوادر الأصول»: الأنبياء زيدوا في النكاح لفضل تنورهم وذلك أن النور إذا امتلأ به الصدر منه وفاض في العروق التذت النفس والعروق فأثارت الشهوة

With this quotation I introduced my book to you, to show you how important sexuality and sex as a physical act in the religion of Islam is.

It is so important to the point, that your belief or faith is measured by how many times you would be able to have intercourse.

The Qur'an encouraged the Muhammadans to engage in sexual relationships with a total of four women at the same time and this is according to the Muhammadans' understanding today, which is considered as marriage by Muslims:

Qur'an 4:3 And, in case you fear that you will not act equitably towards the orphans, then marry such women as is good to you, two, three, four, (Literally: in twos and threes and fours) then, in case you fear that you will not do justice, then one (only), or what your right hands possess. That (way) is likelier you will not be in want (Or: you will have too many dependents). Translation of Dr. Ghali

When we question that issue, which appears in Qur'an 4:3 immediately you will get tons of answers but none of them comes with any logic specially when we ask the following questions:

- How an adult can marry an orphan, the word orphan means a child and his/her parents passed away, so in order to be good to a child you should have sex with him or her?
- The verse did not say have sex (or get married) with up to four women but the total is nine, because the verses are clearly "twos and threes and fours", 2+3+4 = 9 and that explains why many of the companions of Muhammad had up to nine women.
- Qur'an 4:3 is adding the condition to be fair to women, which means between them *"in case you fear that you will not do justice, then one (only)"*, but yet this is contradicting another verse in the same chapter.
  - *Qur'an 4:129 And you will never be able to do justice between (your) wives, (Literally: women) even if you are (so) eager; yet do not incline away completely (Literally: incline away all inclining) (from one), so that you leave her (behind) as if she were suspended. And in case you (do) righteousness and are pious (to Allah), then surely Allah has been Ever-Forgiving, Ever-Merciful.* (translation of Dr. Muhammad Ghali)

As usual Muhammad is the champion of contradiction, in his very own words which supposedly he claimed to be the "words of God", in Qur'an 3:7 he said: there is a huge part of my book no one knows what it means save Allah, and that was a statement made by him in order to answer the accusation of being a false prophet because he says things he himself cannot explain, so the excuse is "only Allah Knows it's meaning" and what makes it more funny is that supposedly this is an answer coming from Allah himself.

Qur'an 3: 7 He it is Who has sent down to thee the Book: In it are verses basic or fundamental (of established meaning); they are the foundation of the Book: others are allegorical. But those in whose hearts is perversity follow the part thereof that is allegorical, seeking discord, and searching for its hidden meanings, but no one knows its hidden meanings except Allah. And those who are firmly grounded in knowledge say: "We believe in the Book; the whole of it is from our Lord:" and none will grasp the Message except men of understanding. Translation of Yusuf Ali

You might notice that I am using translations made by Muslims, in fact I don't approve any of the translations but I'm using their own words to avoid any accusation of "false" translation, because this is what Muhammadans always do to answer me.

All the stories and the lifestyle of Muhammad are overwhelming. Full of contradictions, hypocrisy, drama, and sometimes very funny comedy even though it wasn't meant to be so, as an example when Muhammad aka Allah speaks of science, saying: and if women have an orgasm first the baby would be a girl, if it is the man who had an orgasm first the baby would be a boy.

(A Jewish man said) I have come to ask you about the child. He (the Prophet) said: The water of man is white, and The water of woman yellow, and when they have sexual intercourse and the male's water cum first upon the female's water, it is the male child that is created by Allah's Decree, and when the water of the female cum first upon the water of the male, a female child is formed by the Decree of Allah. The Jew said: What you have said is true; verily you are an Apostle. He then returned and went away. The Messenger of Allah said: He asked me about such and such things of which I have had no knowledge till Allah gave me that. Sahih Muslim 315 a

And you need to take into consideration that all the reference about Muhammad, is collected, written and printed by Muslims themselves, and that was after long filtering and selective processes in order to make him look as the best man, so imagine how ugly the truth would be without filtering!

However, the process of defending Muhammad never stops: in the year 2008 the president of Turkey, Erdogan invited Muslim scholars from around the world, with as purpose to filter the references and Hadith about Muhammad, and I am sure again in a few years from now they would have a new conference to do more filtering.

And a filtering process is nothing but evidence that Muslims are truly unhappy about the heritage of their self-proclaimed prophet, and the only way to save his reputation, is to delete all the stories written in their books.

And the funny thing is, the amount of stories which they don't like is almost 90%.

Search for this article to read more about this topic **"Turkish scholars aim to modernize Islam's Hadith"**, however the Muslims were being called for the same kind of conference, in 2012, 2013, 2014, 2015, 2016 and 2017.

Yet the followers and the supporters of the dictator Erdogan, that are fighting to filter Muhammad's life stories they themselves are willing to fabricate hadiths about Muhammad stating how they would win that election.

Pro-Erdogan columnist makes up hadith claims Prophet signaled that "they will win the Apr 16 referendum" source turkishjournal.com.

After this introduction, we will use only reference which was and still is approved by the vast majority of Muslims around the world.

Those references were agreed upon for the last 12 centuries, and do you know that during this long period of time, all the major Islamic sects used it without ever questioning their legitimacy.

But the era of the internet turned out to be a major element of education and news, however only about 1% of Muhammadans' books are published on the internet, and those who speak Arabic like me and many others, are able to use the internet to expose the cult of Islam from its own books. In the year 1998 I was introduced to the internet for the first time, and ever since my journey with exposing Islam, expanded from local exposure to a worldwide audience. So, let us learn the truth, and I would like to ask all of you to examine every reference I am going to provide in my book, and I assure you will find nothing but total accuracy.

We are born from the shoulder of Adam or sex?

As long as we are talking about sexuality and marriage, we'd better know from now on, Islam is the most confusing religion and this is an example of that.

It is a common sense that we human beings believe even if you are an atheist, that we are and I mean me and you and everybody, the product of sexual relationship regardless if it is it from a legal marriage or not.

Yet the prophet of Islam has a different story to deliver.

Narrated Abu Hurairah: *that the Messenger of Allah said: "When Allah created Adam He sponged his back and every human that He created among his offspring until the Day of Resurrection fell out of his back. He placed a ray of light between the eyes of every person. Then He showed them to Adam and he said: 'O Lord! Who are these people?' He said: 'These are your offspring.' He saw one of them whose ray between his eyes amazed him, so he said: 'O Lord! Who is this?' He said: 'This is a man from the latter nations of your offspring called Dawud.' He said: 'Lord! How long did You make his lifetime?' He said: 'Sixty years.' He said: 'O Lord! Add forty years from my life to his.' So at the end of Adam's life, the Angel of death of came to him, and he said: 'Do I not have forty years remaining?' He said: 'Did you not give them to your son Dawud?'" He said: "Adam denied, so his offspring denied, and Adam forgot and his offspring forgot, and Adam sinned, so his offspring sinned."*

Jami` at-Tirmidhi Vol. 5, Book 44, Hadith 3076

I am sure you noticed right away, how funny this his story is!

- According to Muhammad we are created in the same day Adam was created.
- We are not created from sexual relationship between Adam and Eve, but because Allah hit Adam in his shoulder! Which is a contradiction to Qur'an 25:54
- So I wonder what was the creation of Eve for? and my mother and your mother?
- Then "we Allah's creation" had been placed in front of Adam on the same day.
- Imagine how many billions from the human race already died and how many would die in the future, yet Adam was able to recognize each and every one of us!
- And there is one guy only his eyes were so amazing and his name is David!
- I am so surprised that his name is not Muhammad!!!
- I am sure there's something wrong with the vision of Adam, however according to Islam there's no one better than Muhammad as all Islamic resources are suggesting, so how come Adam's attention was for David only and he did not notice Muhammad?
- He claimed that we can borrow years from each other's lifespan, I am not sure if I can borrow some 20 years from my grandfather Adam so I can live longer or let's say 200 years!
- It sounds like a story fit for kindergarten kids.

As you see we are not speaking about religion teaching science or logic or even common sense but teaching funny fiction. But who dares to laugh at the fairytale stories made up by Muhammad! Well I do, and nothing will stop me from doing so until I die.

However, it didn't take Muhammad long to change his mind about how we are created, based on the coming story we are created from Adam and Eve, in addition to that Muhammad taught his followers that the urine of the female is always mixed with blood!

It was narrated from 'Ali that: *The Prophet said concerning the urine of a nursing infant: "Water should be sprinkled over the urine of a boy, and the urine of a girl should be washed."* Abu Al-Hasan bin Salamah said: "Ahmad bin Musa bin Ma'qil narrated to us that Abul-Yaman Al-Misri said: 'I asked Shafi'i about the Hadith of the Prophet, "Water should be sprinkled over the urine of a baby boy, and the urine *of a baby girl should be washed,"* when the two types of water (urination) are the same. He said, *"This is because the urine of the boy is of water and clay, but the urine of the girl is of flesh and blood."* Then he said to me: *"Did you understand?"* I said: *"No."* He said: *"When Allah the Most High created Adam, He created Eve (Hawwa') from his short rib, so the boy's urine is from water and clay, and the girl's urine is from flesh and blood."* Then he said to me: *"Did you understand?"* I said: *"Yes."* He said: *"May Allah cause you benefit from this."* Sunan Ibn Majah Vol. 1, Book 1, Hadith 525

And the Qur'an has different story!

Qur'an 16: 4 He has created man from Nu'tfah (mixed drops of male and female sexual discharge), then behold, this same (man) becomes an open opponent.

Mohsin Khan translation

From the previous verse we understand that Muhammad teaches us that both women and men have sperm! However for further details I advise you to read my two other books, the Deception of Allah, and Qur'an & Science In Depth.

SEXUALITY BEFORE ISLAM

Before we understand what Islam's point of view of Sexuality is, we'd better form us an idea of sexuality in the pre-Islamic era.

You will be very surprised by the coming information you will learn today. There were many kinds of sexual relationships practiced before Islam, which is a very clear proof for freedom of sexuality sometimes beyond imagination, and I will share with you some of them.

Nika'h meaning

The meaning of the word Nikah, simply means sex, intercourse.

However, Muslims in most translations translate it as marriage and for sure that is false. If we go to the official government site of ministry of Islam in Algeria we will find this question "what about a man did Nika'h to an Animal" so if Nika'h means marriage does that mean Muslims can marry goats? حكم من نكح بهيمة

And from a Muslim official site we quote: *"In Islam, marriage is not restricted to a platonic relationship between husband and wife, nor is it solely for procreation. The Islamic term for marriage, "nikah" literally means sexual intercourse."* al-islam.org

But the reason Muslims are trying to deny that is, because they feel ashamed that their religion does not describe marriage in other words besides the F*** word, which is a clear evidence of the savagery of the founder of Islam.

THE KINDS OF NIKA'H BEFORE ISLAM

From the mouth of 'Aisha

Narrated 'Urwa bin Al-Zubair: *'Aisha, the wife of the Prophet (Allah pray on him and salute him) told him that there were four types of Nika'h during Pre-Islamic period of Ignorance. One type was similar to that of the present day i.e. a man used to ask somebody else for the hand of a girl under his custody or for his daughter's hand and give her money and then marry her. The second type was that a man would say to his wife after she had become clean from her period: "Send for so-and-so and have sexual intercourse with him." Her husband would then keep himself from her and would never sleep with her till she got pregnant from the other man with whom she was sleeping. When her pregnancy became obvious, he the husband would sleep with her again if he wished. Her husband did so (i.e. let his wife sleep with some other man) for the purpose of having a child of noble breed. Such marriage was called as Al-Istibda'. Another type of Nika'h was that a group of less than ten men would gather and enter upon a woman, and all of them would have a sexual relation with her. If she became pregnant and delivered a child and some days had passed after delivery, she would send for all of them and none of them would refuse to come, and when they all gathered before her, she would say to them, "You (all) know what you have done, and now I have given birth to a child. So, it is your child so-and-so!" naming whoever she wished, and her child would follow him and he could not refuse to take him. The fourth type of Nika'h was that many people would enter upon a lady and she would never refuse anyone who came to her. Those were the prostitutes who used to fix flags at their doors as sign, and he who wished, could have sexual intercourse with them. If anyone of them got pregnant and delivered a child, then all those men would be gathered for her and they would call the 'Qafa (which is a person skilled in recognizing the likeness of a child to his father) and would let the child follow the man (whom they acknowledged as his father) and she would let him follow him to be called his son. The man would not refuse all that. But when Muhammad was sent with the Truth, he abolished all the types of Nika'h observed in pre-Islamic period of Ignorance except the type of Nika'h the people recognize today (as Muslims).* Sahih al-Bukhari 5127

However, in this hadith 'Aisha, the wife of Muhammad, did not include all sorts of sexual contracts, yet she was using the word Nika'h, while in Muslims' translation, the word Nika'h appears as marriage which is absolutely false.

Nika'h AL-Mubadalah

نكاح البدل

One of the most famous Arab sexual traditions at that time, was the practice of switching or exchanging wives.

So, if a neighbor was bored with his wife and his wife was bored with him they could ask someone of their choice to exchange wives for a few days or a few months for a pre-agreed period. That surely is purely for sexual pleasure without any intention of marriage.

Nika'h Al- ISTIBDA'

نكاح الأستبضاع

In this kind of sexual relationship, the husband would look for a high standard person, like a warrior, a poet, or noble man, and he would ask him to accept taking his wife to his house and to sleep with her until she got pregnant, and the purpose of this relationship is to enhance the quality of the husband's children.

Nika'h Al Mu'damada

نكاح المضامدة

In this kind of sexual relationship, the women could add anytime a new husband to the first one she was married to, and most likely it was an action which Arabian women used to do, to create kind of jealousy, or to punish her first husband who she is still married to.

Nika'h AL-Mu'khadnah

نكاح المخادنة

This kind of relationship is very close to what is called in the west mistress, however the Quran spoke of it:

Today I made lawful for you. The food of those who have received the Scripture is lawful for you, and your food is lawful for them. And so are the righteous women of the believers and the righteous women of those who received the Scripture before you (lawful for you) when ye give them their wages and live with them in honor, not in fornication, nor taking them as secret concubines. Whoso denieth the faith, his work is vain and he will be among the losers in the Hereafter. Quran 5:5

However, this kind of practice can be considered as cheating and is not a practice that is publicly approved like the other practices I mentioned previously.

Women with the flag

This is something that exists until now in every corner of this earth. It is literally a group of prostitutes, or one running a prostitution business, she puts on top of her house a flag, usually red, which is a sign of the kind of the business she's doing so the "customers" would be informed of where she is located.

Nika'h Al-shu'gar

نكاح الشغار

This practice usually, is very simple, "You give me your daughter and I give you mine" for sexual purposes, it's like the exchange of goods, without using money which would make it very easy to practice for two men having no money whatsoever.

THE KINDS OF MARRIAGE BEFORE ISLAM

Zawaj Al-ma'qet

زواج المقت

The world Zawaj means marriage, and you might notice with me, that in the list previously mentioned we used the word Nika'h which literally means intercourse, in Zawaj Al-Ma'qet. When the father of the family would pass away, his son, usually his oldest, would marry the widow of the father, and usually this kind of practice was not meant for sexual purposes, but to avoid losing the money of the father in case his widow would decide to leave after his death.

Zawaj Al-Rah't

زواج الرهط

This kind of sexual relationship, is based on a the group of men all sharing one woman, the maximum number of husbands should not exceed 10, and when she got pregnant, the woman would inform all the husbands and when a baby was born she would choose amongst them the father, and all the men would have to accept her choice with no argument whatsoever and this is the kind of marriage the mother of Muhammad had as I explained my book "The Deception of Allah".

At the end of this summary about the sexual practice on the Arabian Peninsula, we noticed that nothing is mentioned about one man getting married to many women as a general practice, because in fact it was the opposite, it was the women who had many choices of sexual practices approved by the community except that one called the mistress.

So when Islam came, it switched the power of sexuality from the control of the women, to be controlled by men, where the man became superior, it's he who makes the choice concerning marriage and divorce, and the only obligation for the man, forced upon him by Islamic law is to be the provider and by that is meant the provider of food, clothing and shelter etc.

KINDS OF NIKA'H IN ISLAM INTERCOURSE CONTRACTS

Before we start speaking of sexuality and Islam, I would like to take you on a journey, to explore "marriage" in Islam, however I don't believe that "Islamic marriage" is qualified to be considered as marriage and for sure I will show you why.

It's true that this religion forbids all the previously mentioned kinds of marriages, except one. However, we are going to examine the structure of marriage in Islam, so we can have a better idea about the social life of the followers of this religion.

When we speak about marriage what will come to our mind as a definition, that it is a relationship between a man and a woman based on the law of society or religious belief system.

And to understand the position about female in the Muhammadans' religion we'd better read and think carefully about the following speech made in the earliest time of Islam:

From the book of Rudat Al-Wa'zen the truthful peace upon him said: a man he complained to the caliph (Ali Muhammad's cousin) about his wives therefore he stood up and he made a speech saying: O people don't be obedient to women in any matter, and don't trust them over your money or over your children, for if you leave it to them, they will lead you into disaster and death, we've found that they don't have god fearing when they are in need, and they have no patience when they are influenced by desire, spending money is a must for them even if they are old, and you will be surprised with them even when they are very old, they are not thankful for you if you give them much and you hold from them little, they will not remember you're good and they memorize the evil, they compete on lying, and they exaggerate with the abuse and unjust, and they compete with the devil, so be careful with them and teach them good so that might do good! Makarem Al-Akhlaq 203

من كتاب روضة الواعظين قال الصادق عليه‌السلام : شكا رجل إلى أمير المؤمنين عليه‌السلام نساءه ، فقام خطيباً ، فقال : معاشر الناس لا تطيعوا النساء على كل حال ولا تأمنوهن على مال ولا تذروهن يدبرن أمر العيال ، فإنهن إن تركن وما أردن أوردن المهالك وعدون أمر المالك ، فإنا وجدناهن لا ورع لهن عند حاجتهن ولا صبر لهن عند شهوتهن ، البذخ لهن لازم وإن كبرن ، والعجب بهن لاحق وإن عجزن ، لا يشكرن الكثير إذا منعن القليل ، ينسين الخير ويحفظن الشر ، يتهافتن بالبهتان ويتمادين بالطغيان ويتصدين للشيطان ، فداروهن على كل حال وأحسنوا لهن المقال لعلهن يحسن الفعال.

I am not going to make any comment about this evil speech, but I think you have an idea how the Islamic view on women is.

Another thing, the most important thing about women in Islam is not her, it is her ability of giving babies, and we know very well how racist this cult is:

The Prophet stood up and made a speech and he said: "you better know that is a black woman she was delivering babies is better than a beautiful woman whom is barren" Makarem Al-Akhlaq 203

وقال صلى الله عليه وآله وسلم : اعلموا أن المرأة السوداء إذا كانت ولودا أحب إلي من الحسناء العاقر

From the beginning of Islam, Muhammad encourages his men to deliver more babies to increase the numbers of his followers so they can conquer other nations and at the same time he would be proud about the numbers of his followers, and even he told his followers that David the Jewish king has sex with 99 women in one night in order to make all of them pregnant in one night so he can do "Jihad" for the sake of Allah!

After this short introduction we go to the topic of marriage.

Marriage is a very old religious practice, existing in all religions regardless if it is a true religion or a cult.

List of kinds of marriages:

Marriage With The Intention Of Divorce

الزواج بنية الطلاق

In this kind of marriage, the man marries a woman just for entertainment or other benefits, without informing the wife that this is what he's planning for, which is: me spending some time with you without me having to update you. Usually such a marriage is done by businessmen for a change and entertainment, or by students living abroad they marry either for entertainment, papers or visas, however in their heart they are planning to get rid of the wife as soon as they don't need her anymore and this is very legal according to Islam.

Pleasure sex contract or Mut'a

زواج المتعة

This kind of sex contract was practiced during the time of Muhammad, and the order for it is mentioned in chapter 4 :24 and later on we will give a deeper explanation for it.

However, from the name of this marriage you can tell it's just about sex, and the condition for it consists of three:

- The female agrees to provide the male, sexual intercourse according to Islam. The female has to say these following sentences "I gave you the pleasure of myself according the price is named and the date we agreed upon", then the man has to answer by saying "I accept"
- For a pre-agreed period of time, which means the contract has to have an expiring date in order to be lawful, for example you decided how many days or how many hours the sex contract is valid for, and when the date is up there is no need for divorce for the contract is dismissed based on that agreement.
- For a pre-agreed amount of money. Which means they have to make clear how much money the female is going to get paid for the sexual service she is providing, and the payment can be done before sex or after depending on the agreement itself.

This kind of marriage does not need any witnesses or any proof, which makes it very lousy.

Zawaj 'Urfi

الزواج العرفي

This kind of marriage, is an agreement between the male and the female without any official recognition, or governmental registration the most of this kind of marriages used to hide your personal status, in case you're married and your wife is going to check on you to see if you're got married to any other women they will find nothing about you because simply it's not registered, and in most of the cases it's just to have a sexual relationship where there is no obligation.

Zawaj Al Misyar

زواج المسيار

The actual translation for this marriage, would be the easy marriage because the woman gives up all her legal rights, like housing, food, clothing, or paying her money upfront and end of the contract, and that situation would be similar to a day of divorce after which the man wouldn't pay a penny for whatever reason.

Daytime marriage

الزواج النهاري

It's named as daytime because the man or the husband would meet his wife secretly during daytime only, so his other wife would never suspect him to be married because he the husband sleeps at home every night.

And usually this kind of marriage is done by businessmen who have sexual relationships with women who most likely work with them like a secretary or an employee.

However, it's very legal according in Islam, because the husband had the right not to mention his new marriage or to hide it from the previous wife.

Tourist marriage

الزواج السياحي

This sounds so cute, so what is it about? So, if you're a tourist you would like to go abroad and you'd like to preserve yourself from "sin", you can hire women to be a wife providing you with sexual services, for the period of time you would be staying in that country. And the women who would do such sort of sexual relationship or so-called marriage are mostly prostitutes, this is why it's a very popular practice by Muslim Turkish women.

There's only one person behind all this mixed up sexual madness. And I am not expecting that followers behave better than their prophet.

Muhammad according to most Muslims had 15 wives, some references claims 13 altogether. But what is the reason for an old man to keep marrying women?

When he married 'Aisha she was 6 years old while he was 54 and 'Aisha was the third wife on the list. And as we know Islam allowed a man to have four wives at the same time only. Which means Muhammad is out of all the conditions and he is not under the sharia law, in other words, he is above the law. And not only he allows himself to have an unlimited number of women as wives and sex slaves, yet he established something new which was women offering themselves for sexual relationship with Muhammad, supposedly the good woman is the one who offered herself to the prophet, and because she is good she would offer her good private part to the best of men of Muhammad, the vagina hunter. And we will talk about this later in great detail.

Temporary Marriage for the purpose of pilgrimage

This kind of marriage was created to cheat on the system of Islam, and because a Muslim woman is not allowed to travel and do Hajj(pilgrimage) by herself, she would look for a temporary husband to marry her during the trip to Mecca, we will go through more details later in this book.

Prostitution is officially legal in Islam:

A lot of people have the idea that the religion of Muhammad forbids adultery, but in fact it is allowed but under other names like the temporary sex contract. However, there's not even a single verse in the book of the Muhammadans, the Qur'an, that forbids prostitution, quite the opposite, prostitution in Islam is alt lowed but the woman has to be a slave woman working for benefit of her master.

If we ask any Muhammadan if prostitution is forbidden? He would answer by saying, adultery is totally forbidden in Islam! But I did not ask him about adultery, my question was so specific, I am asking about prostitution. There is not even a single word in the whole Qur'an about prostitution except in chapter 24 verse number 33.

To make it simple it's not allowed for Muslim free women to be a prostitute, that is only for slave Muslim women owned by a Muslim even if the slave woman is a Muslim in this case.

This verse according to Islamic books was revealed when Muhammad was weak, and that explains why the coming verse is useless and meaningless, let us read it together

Qur'an 24:33 .... *force not your girls (slaves) to prostitution if they desire chastity, in order that ye may make a gain in the profit of this life. But if anyone forces them, yet, after such compulsion, is Allah, Oft-Forgiving, Most Merciful.*

What I understand right away from this verse is the following:

↬ Force not women into prostitution.
↬ If they don't like to do so and work as a prostitute.

↪ But if they like and if they agree to work as a prostitute, there is no problem!

If you read all Islamic interpretations, you will find all of them agree, that what the verse is saying is that you should not force your Muslim female slaves, and if you force them Allah is forgiving, and the forgiveness here according to some scholars was for the girls, however what about the one who forced them?

Imagine I come to you and you are a person claiming to be prophet of God, and I inform you there is a Muslim forcing his slave girls, and what is your response? Allah forgives the girls?

1. Why he did not say this is forbidden?
2. Why he did not make a punishment for the one who practices this?
3. Why Muhammad did not even say: the one who would do this would go to hell?
4. And remember that verse was a response to Muslim men practicing such a behavior, with Muslim women!
5. But as usual he claims to be the good man of the good God, only he had to compromise, therefore he made the verse, thus making everybody happy except the slaves.
6. There are many verses in the Qur'an forbidding Muslims from some practices, like not to eat eating pork!
7. So the god of Muhammad made it very clear not to eat pork, but prostitution is not a serious issue? No need to say: don't ever practice prostitution? Which topic is more important?
8. All what he said was "Force them not if they choose chastity"
9. In other words, if you like running a pimp business using your Muslim slave girls, it's fine as long as they agree to do so.
10. However, there is no punishment nor a promise of punishment for those who do this to those slaves.
11. At the same time the slave girls were Muslims according to some scholars, and Muhammad had to say something to make the slaves still accept him as a prophet, so he made a verse that didn't upset the feelings of the slave owners, and at the other hand gave the slaves a promise to be forgiving for the sin they were doing!
12. And what about the slave girl if she is non-Muslim?
13. As long as this is a verse about Muslim female slaves, what is the situation for the non-Muslim slave?
14. It's obvious. In the case of non-Muslim there is no problem, regardless if you're Muslim or not, it is lawful to do the business of a pimp.

The fornicator can only have intercourse with another fornicator

Dr Muhammad Ghali Translation: *Qur'an 24:3 The fornicator shall marry none except a female fornicator or a female associator; (i.e., one who associates other with Allah) and the female fornicator, none shall marry her except a fornicator or a (male) associator; (i.e., one who associates other with Allah) and that is prohibited for the believers.*

Again, I'm using an Islamic translation, therefore the Muhammadans cannot say I'm using my own translation.

My translation is the following: *Qur'an 24:3 The fornicator does not have sexual intercourse except a [female] fornicator or polytheist, and none can have sexual intercourse with her except a fornicator or a polytheist, and that has been made unlawful to the believers*

This verse is full of errors and out of logic. We explained before that the word Nikah means sexual intercourse, in all Islamic translation to English they are replacing that word with marry! However, if the word would represent 'marry' look what you're going to find in this verse:

- Fornicator can have sex only with fornicator!
- The verse speaks of two options, one for men and one for the women.
- Option one: if the word Nika'h here is understood as marriage by Muslims, then what if I am a male fornicator, and I converted to Islam, I would not be able to marry a decent woman?
- And this is the logic of the god of Islam?
- So now we are both fornicators and we are going to have a decent family? Or a fornicator Muslim family!
- The second option is, if you're a fornicator and you are a Muslim woman, you are not allowed to marry a Muslim man unless he is a fornicator, or to marry a non-Muslim man?
- Notice that verse said clearly and I will you show the Muslim's translation to prove my point "none shall marry her except a fornicator or a (male) associator; (i.e., one who associates other with Allah)"
- But isn't this a contradiction to the teaching of Islam that you cannot marry a non-Muslim if you are a Muslim woman?
- Even if you're a Muslim man whether currently doing fornication or in your past, can you marry someone being a Buddhist or Hindu?
- That is totally forbidden in the Muhammadans' religion so how can we practice this verse?

↪ When Muhammad took women to bed without marriage, and there's a long list of them, was he a fornicator?

↪ What about those women who offered themselves to the prophet to have sexual intercourse with him, are they fornicators?

↪ As you notice the title of fornicator is very flexible in this cult, and the size of fit stretches out depending on the size of the person. If the person is Muhammad then yes it is very lawful for him to receive women in his bed without marriage and no, that is not fornication!

↪ And one last question, if the word Nikah according to Muslims means marriage, so what kind of society Muhammad is it trying to accomplish? And what is the wisdom of this!

It seems to me that Muhammad is trying to copy the words of Jesus Christ, but from his mouth it came very stupid after he played with the words, because as we know divorce in Islam is very easy, and actually there is no marriage it is just a sex contract.

Matthew 19:9 And I say unto you, whosoever shall put away his wife, except it be for fornication, and shall marry another, committeth adultery: and whoso marrieth her which is put away doth commit adultery.

You do not need to be a genius to see the huge differences between the holiness of Christ, and the corruption of Muhammad.

Creating verses to make himself appear as if he is against adultery when in fact he is the first fornicator.

Homosexual Imam seducing the Muhammadans

What we should do if our prayer leader is a gay and horny!

Narrated 'Ubaid-Ullah bin Adi bin Khiyar: *I went to 'Uthman Iben 'Affan while he was overwhelmed, and said to him, "You are the chief of all Muslims in general and you see what has occurred you. We are led in the prayer by a leader of Fitan (temptation and afflictions etc.) and we are afraid of being sinful in following him." 'Uthman said. "the prayers is the best of all deeds so when the people do good deeds do the same with them and when they do bad deeds, avoid those bad deeds." Al-Zuhri said, "I see that there is no choice but to pray behind a homosexual Imam." Sahih al-Bukhari 695*

The homosexual caliph

'Umar Ibn Al-'Kha'tab He succeeded Abu Bakr as the second caliph, but let us explore this Caliph sexual life together.

Book of Nur Al-Anwar Fe Shareh Al Sa'hefa Al-Sujadiah Page 7

And Al-mubashe said in his Tafsir(interpretation) for the statement of Al-sadeq peace up on him(grandson of Muhammad) that there's no one was named with such a title(the leader of the believers) except Ali Bin Abi 'Talib peace up on him except the one who was a homosexual, this is similar to the statement of Imam Jalal Al-Deen Al-Sou'ty and he is one of their biggest scholars(Muslim suni) in his comment on the dictionary Tashih Al-Lugah Al 'Abinah, and it was a group in the pre-Islamic era one of them is our master 'Umar and this is what was said by Ibn Al-Athir and he is one of their greatest scholars(he meant the Muslim suni) he said: Al-Rawafid(the Shia Muslims) said: that our master 'Umar was a homosexual, they told a lie may Allah curse them, what he had was a sickness it's cool down by the water of man(sperm of men).

نور الأنوار في شرح الصحيفة السجادية

و قد روى العياشي في تفسيره حديثا،عن الصادق عليه السلام،بأنه لم يسم أحد بهذا الاسم غير علي بن أبي طالب عليه السلام إلا كان مخنثا،و هو غير بعيد،لقول جلال الدين السيوطي و هو من أكابر علمائهم،في تعاليقه على القاموس،عند تصحيح لغة الأبنة،و كانت في جماعة في زمن الجاهلية أحدهم سيدنا عمر،و قول ابن الأثير،و هو أيضا من أعظم فضلائهم.زعمت الروافض أن سيدنا عمر كان مخنثا،كذبوا لعنهم الله،و لكن كان به داء دواؤه ماء الرجال.فانظر إلى اعتذار هذا الفاضل عن إمامه،

I apologize the translation to English maybe it's kind of confusing for you, but the original text in Arabic is horrible to translate and I did my best to keep it close to the original.

However, this is a fight between the Muslim Shia and Sunni, where that Muslim Shia are supposedly using some quotation from Muslim Sunni, where the Muslim Sunni scholar accuses the Shia of lying, but at the same time he admits that the caliph 'Umar has a disease in his anus and is claiming to use the sperm of men to cool that down!

The Muslim Shia has a stronger reason to believe that 'Umar was a homosexual using the following Sunni sect hadith

Narrated Ibn 'Abbas: *The Prophet cursed effeminate men (those men who are in the similitude (act like women) and those women who assume the manners of men, and he said, "Turn them out of your houses." The Prophet turned out such-and-such man, and 'Umar turned out such-and-such people(gays). Sahih al-Bukhari 6834*

So, the Shia they Ask the Muslims Sunni what the gays were doing in the house of 'Umar?

And I ask the Shia don't you see that your prophet himself, kicked gays from his house too? So, they are trying to prove that 'Umar was a gay because he had gays in his house, but they are not questioning why the prophet had gays in his house?

I am not a homosexual like caliph Yazid

History books written by Muslims exposed also a lot of the sexual history of the Islamic caliphs and I chose some of the more important ones.

Abd al-Malik, fifth caliph (685–705) He made the famous speech, presenting himself as warrior of his family and Muhammad paid his family a lot of money in order to accept him as a prophet, as it is written in the chapter Qur'an *9:60 "and those in debts and in the way of Allah and the wayfarer"*, however in his speech he revealed a lot of things about previous caliphs:

"I am not like the weak caliphate and he meant 'Uthman, the caliphate the fornicator and he meant Mu'awiya and not like that the caliphate the homosexual and he meant Yzid" The history of Islam page 461, and Tareekh Khalifah 171, and Al-Kamel for Ibn Al-Athir 4/391, and Tareekh al Ya'qubi 2/274

فإنّي لست بالخليفة المستضعف (يعني عثمان) ولا بالخليفة المداهن (يعني معاوية) ولا بالخليفة المأفون (يعني يزيد) ! ألا وإنّي لا أداوي هذه الأُمّة إلاّ بالسيف حتّى تستقيم لي قناتكم !

The caliph 'Uthman's father was a homosexual!

Book of Mathaleb Al-Arab chapter of adulteress and homosexuality Page 36. *Reported by Hisham from his father he said: from those who they used to play with(F***) and a homosexual was Abd-Allah Abu 'Tal'ha son of Abd-allah son of 'Uthman bin 'Umar bin Ka'eb ..and 'Afan bin Al-'Aass Bin 'Umayiah*

هشام عن أبيه قال: كان ممن يلعب به ويتخنث عبد الله أبو طلحة بن عبد الله بن عثمان بن عمرو بن كعب، وولده بالمدينة(و) والكوفة، وعفان بن أبي العاص بن أمية

The Uncle of Muhammad 'Abbas bin 'Abd Al Mu'talib was a gay!

We do not need to look over many books to find out how the sexual practices of the people of Mecca used to be, and I think it is still the same. As an example, from the book of AL-Ma'thalib by Imam Al-Siri who died in 204 Islamic year, the book authenticated by Dr. Rana Muhammad the head of Islamic studies in the Punjab.

This is a book made by Muslim scholars and the copy I am using is from the university of Lahore Pakistan. I found that most of the companions and relatives of Muhammad were homosexual, remember the tribe of Qurish is a small tribe and based on Islamic resources this community was a homosexual and bisexual community.

The chapter back door F***(anus). Report by Hisham from his father that from the list of names which was accused of being homosexual .... (Long list) and it's also was reported that 'Abbas Ibn Abid Al-Mu'talib was one of the homosexuals.

Book of AL-Ma'thalib by Imam Al-Siri page 36. Printed copy 1977 university of Lahore Pakistan. Take a note 'Abbas Ibn Abid Al-Mu'talib is the direct uncle for Muhammad the son of his grandfather Abid Al-Mu'talib.

عن) هشام عن أبيه قال : كان ممن يتهم باللواطة كرز بن ربيعة بن حبيب، جد عبد الله بن عامر))
بن كرز (1) وولده بالبصرة والبناج، وحاطب بن عمرو (2) أخو سهيل بن عمرو له صحبة، ولا عقب
له ، والعقب لأخيه سهيل بالمدينة، ويقال: إن سهيلاً لا عقب له أيضا.
وهشام بن عبد الله بن أبي قيس من بني عامر بن لؤي، وهو أبو وهيب جد ابن أبي ذؤيب المحدث،
مات في الإسلام، ويقال: إن العباس بن عبد المطلب كان أحد اللاطة (3)، والله أعلم.
عبد الله بن عامر والي عثمان على البصرة، وقد ساهم في حرب الجمل في صفوف عائشة، ثم (1)
أصبح في حزب معاوية * تاريخ ابن عساكر 482/21، 285، أسد الغابة 3/ 288
قال الرازي هو حاطب بن عمرو بن عبد شمس من المهاجرين الأولين* الجرح والتعديل ، الرازي (2)
3/ 303، عيون ا لأثر ، ابن سيد الناس 1/ 151

And from the book of Nur Al-Qabas volume 1 Page 68 by Imam Murzbani summarized by Imam Al-Yagmuri Page 183. *And Al-Mad'ani said: 'Afan Ibn Al-'Ass(1) was a feminine and he used to play the drums for wedding parties, and Al'Hakam bin Al-'Ass(2) was the same and Shibah was throat guy(blowjob), and he used to be F*** by Munabih Ibn Al'Ajaj bin Sa'ed bin Sahem, and also Abu Jahl Ibn Hisham(3), And Al-Nu'dar bin Al-'Harith bin 'Alqimah was throat guy(blowjob), and he used to be F*** by Safwan bin 'Amuiah bin Khalaf(4), and Khalid bin*

Khuelid bin Hazim was a feminine and he used to be F*** by Rabi'ah bn Al-'Harith bin Abid Al-Mu'talib(5), and 'Anbasa bun Abi 'A'Hi'ha Sa'id Ibn Al-'Ass was throat guy(blowjob), and Mus'ab Ibn Al-Zuibir(6) was a feminine and 'Abid Al 'Aziz Bin Marwan throat guy(blowjob)(7), and he was drunk man. And Yazid Bin 'Abd Al-Malik(8) his mother 'Atikah daughter of Yazid of Mu'awiah he was feminine throat guy(blowjob), And Al-Walid bin 'Abd Al-Malik was a throat guy(blowjob) and drunk(9), and he was drunk man And Jamil Bin Ma'hfuz Al-Azadi...

وقال المدائني: كان عفان بن أبي العاص مؤنثا يلعب في الأعراس بالدف، ومثله الحكم بن أبي العاص، وكان شيبة بن ربيعة حلقيا وكان يأتيه منبه بن الحجاج بن سعد بن سهم وكذلك أبو جهل بن هشام، وكان النضر بن الحارث بن علقمة حلقيا ويأتيه صفوان بن أمية بن خلف، وكان خالد بن خويلد بن حزام مؤنثا ويأتيه ربيعة بن الحارث بن عبد المطلب، وكان عنبسة بن أبي أحيحة سعيد بن العاص حلقيا، وكان مصعب بن الزبير مؤنثا، وكان عبد العزيز بن مروان حلقيا محدودا في خمر، وكان يزيد بن عبد الملك - وهو ابن عاتكة بنت يزيد بن معاوية - حلقيا، وكان الوليد بن يزيد بن عبد الملك حلقيا مؤنثا، وكان ألحوص بن محمد مستوها، ويزيد بن المهلب وقبيصة بن المهلب حلقيان، وكان يزيد بن حاتم مخنثا حلقيا، وجميل بن محفوظ الأزدي مستوها، وكان خالد بن عبد الله القسري حلقيا مستوها، وكان سفيان بن معاوية بن يزيد ابن المهلب حلقيا مشهورا بذلك، وكان محمد بن القاسم بن محمد بن الحكم

All these names considered as part of the family of Qathem aka prophet Muhammad.

1. 'Afan Ibn Al-'Ass is the father of the third caliph in Islam!, plus his brother
2. Al'Hakam bin Al-'Ass, both were homosexual.
3. Abu Jahl Ibn Hisham was a homosexual, but yet Muhammad invoked his god to make him Muslim!

Narrated Ibn 'Umar: *that the Messenger of Allah said: "O Allah! Honor Islam through the most dear of these two men to you: Through Abu Jahl or through 'Umar bin Al-Khattab." He said: "And the most dear of them to Him was 'Umar."* Jami` at-Tirmidhi Vol. 1, Book 46, Hadith 3681

4. Safwan bin 'Amuiah bin Khalaf named by Muhammad as a leader for hundreds of soldiers but yet is a homosexual!
5. Al-'Harith bin Abid Al-Mu'talib was a direct uncle to Muhammad but yet a homosexual!
6. Mus'ab Ibn Al-Zuibir he is the son of one of Muhammad companions, and the brother of caliph Abdulah Ibn Al-Zuibir, yet he is a homosexual
7. 'Abid Al 'Aziz Bin Marwan the governor of Egypt! And he was King of Egypt for more than 20 years, mentioned as homosexual
8. Yazid Bin 'Abd Al-Malik he was a king and the caliph but but yet homosexual
9. Al-Walid bin 'Abd Al-Malik he was a caliph but yet homosexual.

10. Khuelid bin Hazim he is one of Muhammad's cousins. And he is homosexual.

We found all of this in one page, do we need more reference to prove what kind of sexual society we are talking about!

MUHAMMAD'S SEXUALITY

I use to ask myself the question why sexuality is so important as a topic, and in fact represents the main core of the Islamic religion.

And one of the major findings strikingly shocking me is the sexual behavior of a man, supposedly at least for those who follow him, the best man ever.

So, let us examine together some of Muhammad's stories, not reported by the enemies of Muhammad but 100% reported by Muslims themselves.

The special privileges of the prophet from Allah

Please take a note that the coming title would say: 16 privileges, however you will notice our amount here exceeds 16, so don't think of this as a mistake, on the contrary, it is just an honest translation from my side.

The 16 privileges Muhammad given by Allah according to the interpretation of Tafsir Al-Qurtbi. Tafsir Al-Qurtbi page 423: 16 privileges of things that were made lawful for the prophet only:

1. The best of the booty.
2. Special privilege one fifth of the war booty for his pocket alone.
3. He fast more!
4. The license from Allah to have more than 4 wives.
5. To F*** any woman as a gift.
6. To F*** a woman without her family permission (of a male family member).
7. To F*** a women without paying money.
8. To have sex (with his wives or with others) during the Haj (pilgrimage).
9. It's lawful for him to break his oath or promise toward his wives.
10. If the eyes of the prophet fall upon a woman, it is an immediate obligation to her husband to divorce her, So the prophet can F*** her, Ibn Al 'Arabi

said: "this is what was said the case of Zinab." (she was the wife of his son, Muhammad flirted with her, and then he took his own son's wife by forcing him to divorce her)

11. He freed Safia instead of paying her.
12. He is allowed to enter Mecca without the needs to perform the rituals Muslims should do.
13. He is allowed to kill in Mecca.
14. Nobody is allowed to inherit him.
15. His wives should be staying married to him even after his death (which means they cannot remarry after becoming his widow).
16. If he divorces one of his wives, she cannot marry a new husband until she dies. (For she is still considered the wife of Muhammad).
17. It is lawful for the prophet to take away the food and drinks from the hungry and thirsty.
18. It is allowed for him to be protected (above the law).
19. Allah made for him lawful all war booty's.
20. He was victorious by terror, and his enemies fear him from a distance of a month.

تفسير القرطبي ص 425

وأما ما أحل له صلى الله عليه وسلم فجملته ستة عشر : الأول : صفي المغنم . الثاني : الاستبداد بخمس الخمس أو الخمس . الثالث : الوصال . الرابع : الزيادة على أربع نسوة . الخامس : النكاح بلفظ الهبة . السادس : النكاح بغير ولي . السابع : النكاح بغير صداق . الثامن : نكاحه في حالة الإحرام . التاسع : سقوط القسم بين الأزواج عنه ، وسيأتي . العاشر : إذا وقع بصره على امرأة وجب على زوجها طلاقها ، وحل له نكاحها . قال ابن العربي : هكذا قال إمام الحرمين ، وقد مضى ما للعلماء في قصة زيد من هذا المعنى . الحادي عشر : أنه أعتق صفية وجعل عتقها صداقها . الثاني عشر : دخول مكة بغير إحرام ، وفي حقنا فيه اختلاف . الثالث عشر : القتال بمكة . الرابع عشر : أنه لا يورث . وإنما ذكر هذا في قسم التحليل لأن الرجل إذا قارب الموت بالمرض زال عنه أكثر ملكه ، ولم يبق له إلا الثلث خالصا ، وبقي ملك رسول الله صلى الله عليه وسلم على ما تقرر بيانه في آية المواريث ، وسورة (مريم) بيانه أيضا . الخامس عشر : بقاء زوجيته من بعد الموت . السادس عشر : إذا طلق امرأة تبقى حرمته عليها فلا تنكح . وهذه الأقسام الثلاثة تقدم معظمها مفصلا في مواضعها . وسيأتي . إن شاء الله تعالى

وأبيح له عليه الصلاة والسلام أخذ الطعام والشراب من الجائع والعطشان ، وإن كان من هو معه يخاف على نفسه الهلاك ، لقوله تعالى : النبي أولى بالمؤمنين من أنفسهم . وعلى كل أحد من المسلمين أن يقي النبي صلى الله عليه وسلم بنفسه . وأبيح له أن يحمي لنفسه . وأكرمه الله بتحليل الغنائم . وجعلت الأرض له ولأمته مسجدا وطهورا . وكان من الأنبياء من لا تصح صلاتهم إلا في المساجد . ونصر بالرعب ، فكان يخافه العدو من مسيرة شهر .

I'm not going to make a lot of comments about what we learned from this Tafsir Al-Qurtbi quotation, but you will notice how important it is that Muhammad must have special privileges. And 70% is about sexual licenses, the rest about money, and his striking selfishness to the point he forced his wives not to get married after his death, as if they were properties for him to own.

- ↬ Any woman wishing to do so can give herself to the prophet, so he can enjoy her.
- ↬ If his eyes fall upon a woman then her husband must divorce her immediately, so the prophet can have her.
- ↬ No oath or promise to his wives needs he be held accountable for, nor has he any obligation to fulfill.
- ↬ He can have more than four wives, for he is above the law.
- ↬ I found privilege number 17 extremely disgusting is "It is lawful for the prophet to take away the food and a drink, from the hungry and thirsty."

And as long as we mentioned the story of Zinab, we'd better read something about this story, which explains the sexual behavior and nature of this man, and his principles as a prophet proclaiming himself as the best of mankind.

All the "sexual privileges" we spoke about, were legalized by Muhammad by fabricating Qur'an verses which were supposedly coming from his god Allah, and that was one of the major reasons for Muhammad to establish new laws, fitting his sexual desires. Laws that became obligatory for Muslims, though in fact being Muhammad's personal privileges.

I want my son's wife in my bed. NOW!

This story is reported and approved by all the major Islamic scholars, it is about Muhammad's son by adoption, his name was Zaid, who was married to a very beautiful woman according to the Muslims reference.

Take a note please that there are six writers of Hadith, their books are considered as Sahih (authentic), so if you see a Muslim saying to you this story is not authentic, it is just an attempt to defend the horrible stories about his prophet.

The authors of the Six Books are:

1- Imam al-Bukhaari   2- Imam Muslim   3- Imam Abu Dawood

4- Imam al-Tirmidhi   5- Imam al-Nasaa'I   6- Imaam Ibn Maajah

However, the six previously mentioned book authors are not the only ones considered authentic, besides them there's many more, all of them get their stories about the biography of Muhammad, from the books written long before they did and there are other important books but Muslims favor those six because they went through a lot of filtering.

Narrated 'Aisha: "*If the Messenger of Allah had concealed anything that was revealed to him, then he would have concealed these Ayat: 'When you said to him on whom Allah has bestowed grace (meaning by Islam); and you have done a favor" Hold your wife to yourself, and have fear of Allah." But you did hide in yourself that which Allah will make manifest, you did fear the people whereas Allah had better right that you should fear Him' up to His saying: 'And Allah's rule must be achieved (33:37).' They said: 'He married his wife's son, so Allah revealed: 'Muhammad is not the father of any of your men, but he is the Messenger of Allah and the Last of the Prophets (33:40).' The Messenger of Allah had adopted him(Zaid) as a son when he was little, and he remained being called 'Zaid son Muhammad' until he grew up to adulthood, then Allah revealed: 'Call them by their fathers, then your brothers in religion and those entrusted to you (33:5). (Say) So-and-so, the entrusted to you of this person and this person etc., the brother of so-and-so. 'That is more just with Allah' meaning that doing that is more just to Allah.*" Jami` at-Tirmidhi Vol. 5, Book 44, Hadith 3207

So there's three major things we learned from this story mentioned by 'Aisha:

- ↩ Zaid was an adopted son by Muhammad since he was a child.
- ↩ Everyone used to call him Zaid son of Muhammad even after he was a grown man, and he got married.
- ↩ Additional important issue some of you might not be aware of, adopting little boys was usually done amongst the Arab by those who could not or were unable to have their own.

So, what happened next?

Based on the Islamic source, the prophet once went to visit his own son by adoption Zaid, found his wife home alone, wearing some kind of see-through clothing and the lust of the prophet starts from there.

Tafsir Al-Qurtbi Qur'an volume 14 Page 172: *Muqatil narrated that the prophet married Zainab daughter of Jahsh to Zaid and she stayed with him for a while. Then one day the prophet Allah pray on him and salute him, came to Zaid house and he saw Zainab standing; she was white with a beautiful figure and one of the most perfect women in Quraish. So He Desired Her and said, "Praise and Won-*

drous is Allah the hearts matchmaker." When Zaynab heard the prophet's excitement of her, she relayed it to Zaid who then understood immediately what you should do, Zaid said to the prophet, "O prophet of Allah, allow me to divorce her, for she has become arrogant; seeing herself superior to me and she offends me with her tongue." The prophet replied, "Hold onto your wife and fear Allah." It was said that Allah had sent a wind which lifted up the curtain to reveal Zainab in her room. When the prophet saw her He Desired Her and it delighted Zainab to be desired by the prophet Allah pray on him and salute him. When Zaid returned home, she informed him of what had happened and Zaid was thus determined to divorce her.

فذهب قتادة وابن زيد وجماعة من المفسرين ، منهم الطبري وغيره - إلى أن النبي صلى الله عليه وسلم وقع منه استحسان لزينب بنت جحش ، وهي في عصمة [ص: 172] زيد ، وكان حريصا على أن يطلقها زيد فيتزوجها هو ؛ ثم إن زيدا لما أخبره بأنه يريد فراقها ، ويشكو منها غلظة قول وعصيان أمر ، وأذى باللسان وتعظما بالشرف ، قال له : اتق الله - أي فيما تقول عنها - وأمسك عليك زوجك وهو يخفي الحرص على طلاق زيد إياها . وهذا الذي كان يخفي في نفسه ، ولكنه لزم ما يجب من الأمر بالمعروف . وقال مقاتل : ثم إنه عليه السلام أتى زيدا يوما يطلبه ، فأبصر زينب قائمة ، كانت بيضاء جميلة جسيمة من أتم نساء قريش ، فهويها وقال : سبحان الله مقلب القلوب ! فسمعت زينب بالتسبيحة فذكرتها لزيد ، فطفن زيد فقال : يا رسول الله ، ائذن لي في طلاقها ، فإن فيها كبرا ، تعظم علي وتؤذيني بلسانها ، فقال عليه السلام : أمسك عليك زوجك واتق الله . وقيل : إن الله بعث ريحا فرفعت الستر وزينب متفضلة في منزلها ، فرأى زينب فوقعت في نفسه ، ووقع في نفس زينب أنها وقعت في نفس النبي صلى الله عليه وسلم وذلك لما جاء يطلب زيدا ، فجاء زيد فأخبرته بذلك ، فوقع في نفس زيد أن يطلقها . . وقال ابن عباس : وتخفي في نفسك الحب لها . وتخشى الناس أي تستحييهم

And the lovely story, a Prophet of "Allah" does not offend, and it did not offend the Muslims for the last 1400 years!

In the same page of the previous reference we find this: "and it always was been said, Zaid son of Muhammad until Allah send down chapter 33: 38"

"Behold! Thou didst say to one who had received the grace of Allah and thy favour: "Retain thou (in wedlock) thy wife, and fear Allah." But thou didst hide in thy heart that which Allah was about to make manifest: thou didst fear the people, but it is more fitting that thou shouldst fear Allah. Then when Zaid had dissolved (his marriage) with her, with the necessary (formality), We joined her in marriage to thee: in order that (in future) there may be no difficulty to the Believers in (the matter of) marriage with the wives of their adopted sons, when the latter have dissolved with the necessary (formality) (their marriage) with them. And Allah's command must be fulfilled." Yusf Ali translation.

فلم يزل يقال : زيد بن محمد إلى أن نزل قوله تعالى : ادعوهم لآبائهم ونزل ما كان محمد أبا أحد م
ن رجالكم .

In the book of the Muslims Shia the Qur'an interpretation Tafsir Nur Al-Tha'qlen volume 4 Page 236: *The messenger of Allah said: " O people of 'Qurish be the witness that Zaid is my son I inherit him and he inherit me", therefore Zaid was always called the son of Muhammad and the messenger of Allah love him and he called him "Zaid of Love" and when the messenger immigrated to the city of Madinah, the prophet married him to Zainab Bint Jahish and one day Zaid did not show up so the messenger came to his house looking for him, and he found Zainab in the middle of her room making mashed gradient then the messenger Allah pray on him and salute him, he pushed the door(to open it more), and immediately he had a crush on her and he said: " praise be to Allah the creator of the light and the blessed is he the best of the creators" and at the moment he had a great place for her and his heart, afterward when Zaid came back home Zainab told him what she heard the messenger saying(flirting), therefore he(Zaid) said: should I divorce you so he can get married to you the messenger of Allah? Perhaps he falls on love with you?*

She said but I'm afraid what if you divorce me and he did not marry me? Therefore, Zaid went to the messenger Allah pray on him and salute him and say to him, O Messenger of Allah I am willing to sacrifice my parents for you, Zainab told me etc. etc. Do you like me to divorce her for you so you can have her?

تفسير نور الثقلين - الشيخ الحويزي - ج ٤ - الصفحة ٢٣٦
فقال رسول الله: اشهدوا ان زيدا ابني أرثه ويرثني، فكان زيد يدعى ابن محمد، وكان رسول الله صلى الله عليه وآله يحبه وسماه زيد الحب، فلما هاجر رسول الله إلى المدينة زوجه زينب بنت جحش وأبطأ عنه يوما، فأتى رسول الله صلى الله عليه وآله منزله يسأل عنه فإذا زينب جالسة وسط حجرتها يسحق طيبها بفهر لها (٢) فدفع رسول الله صلى الله عليه وآله الباب ونظر إليها وكانت جميلة حسنة فقال: سبحان الله خالق النور وتبارك الله أحسن الخالقين، ثم رجع رسول الله إلى منزله ووقعت زينب في قلبه موقعا عجيبا، وجاء زيد إلى منزله فأخبرته زينب بما قال رسول الله صلى الله عليه وآله فقال لها زيد: هل لك ان اطلقك حتى يتزوجك رسول الله فلعلك قد وقعت في قلبه؟فقالت: أخشى أن تطلقني ولا يتزوجني رسول الله، فجاء زيد إلى رسول الله صلى الله عليه وآله فقال: بأبي أنت وأمي يا رسول الله أخبرتني زينب بكذا وكذا فهل لك ان أطلقها حتى تتزوجها؟

You can notice the hypocrisy of Muhammad.

1. I presented to you two stories. The first made by the Muslims Sunni, and the last one by the Muslim Shiah, however both of them do confirm the same scandal.
2. He was flirting with Zaid wife in the morning.
3. But yet he told him fear Allah and hold your wife for yourself at night.
4. Announcing to a married woman his lust and love, saying the words loud on purpose so she can hear it.

5. And we are not sure if this was the conspiracy between him, I mean Muhammad and Zainab the wife of Zaid.

6. Because this whole story does not make sense to me, especially if we add some more information namely Muhammad had been the one who married and chose for Zaid his wife Zainab.

7. And as always, all Muhammad's sex stories end with a happy ending by Allah sending a Quran to help and satisfy the sexual desire of the most beloved prophet to Allah. If we read the verse in the Qur'an carefully, we would notice how Muhammad by his fabrications, claimed that it is his god guiding him to do the right action and I quote, 'Behold! Thou didst say to one who had received the grace of Allah and thy favor: "Retain thou (in wedlock) thy wife, and fear Allah." But thou didst hide in thy heart that which Allah was about to make manifest: thou didst fear the people".

8. Imagine god is asking his prophet: why you are hiding your lust to a married woman?

9. To make it simple, Muhammad made a verse stating this married woman is yours: grab her and don't worry about her husband or the people.

10. And as always, his reason to make a Qur'an verse is just to cover his lust, thus saying this is god's wish not mine!

Was he accused to be a womanizer?

What we are noticing today, was so clear for people who lived around Muhammad at his time.

Qur'an 13:38 stated clearly that accusation.

We did send messengers before thee and appointed for them wives and children: and it was never the part of a messenger to bring a sign except as Allah.

To get more details about this accusation we read:

. (قوله تعالى : (ولقد أرسلنا رسلا من قبلك وجعلنا لهم أزواجا

قال الكلبي : عيرت اليهود رسول الله - صلى الله عليه وسلم - وقالت : ما نرى لهذا الرجل همة - 551

. إلا النساء والنكاح ، ولو كان نبيا كما زعم لشغله أمر النبوة عن النساء ، فأنزل الله تعالى هذه الآية

(And verily We sent messengers (to mankind) before thee, and We appointed for them wives and offspring...) [13:38]. Said al-Kalbi: "The Jews disrespected the Messenger of, Allah pray on him and salute him, saying: 'This man has no objective except for women and sex. If he was really a prophet, as he claims to be, the matter of prophet hood would have preoccupied him from women', and so Allah, exalted is

He, revealed this verse". Asbab Al-Nuzul by Al-Wahidi issue 551

So, Muhammad was telling the Jews do not be hypocrite I am the same as previous prophets like for example David!

But anyone with a only a little knowledge about the Bible, will find right away that David was full of sorrow for the sin he committed, On the contrary, Muhammad is proud about it, and not only that he subsequently claims that this was his God's order the same as it was for previous prophets to have many and unlimited numbers of women.

To understand how David felt about what he did let us read together from the book of Psalm 38:

[15] *For in thee, O Lord, do I hope: thou wilt hear, O Lord my God.* [16] *For I said, hear me, lest otherwise they should rejoice over me: when my foot slippeth, they magnify themselves against me.* [17] *For I am ready to halt, and my sorrow is continually before me.* [18] *For I will declare mine iniquity; I will be sorry for my sin.* [19] *But mine enemies are lively, and they are strong: and they that hate me wrongfully are multiplied. 20 They also that render evil for good are mine adversaries; because I follow the thing that good is.* [21] *Forsake me not, O Lord: O my God, be not far from me. 22 Make haste to help me, O Lord my salvation.*

Jealousy versus stupidity

Some men have extra jealousy over their wives but I find jealousy mostly occurring by men who are feeling insecure, which makes other men existing around their wives appear to them as a threat.

In the coming story there is a great example of Muhammad's mental illness:

Narrated Nabhan the slave of Umm Salamah: *that Umm Salamah told to him, that she and Maimunah were with the Messenger, Allah pray on him and salute him she said: "So when we were with him, Ibn Umm Maktum came, and he entered upon him, and that was after veiling had been ordered for us. So the Messenger Allah pray on him and salute him said: 'Veil yourselves from him.' So, I said: 'O Messenger of Allah! Is he not blind such that he can't see us or recognize us?' So the Messenger Allah pray on him and salute him said: 'Are you two blind such that you can't see him?'"* Jami` at-Tirmidhi Vol. 5, Book 41, Hadith 2778

↤ Muslim women are ordered to cover themselves in front of strange men.

- ✤ However, the purpose of this covering that the man should not see her, they can walk on the streets and see whatever man is walking by.
- ✤ So, what is the point of Muhammad asking his wives to cover themselves for a blind man?
- ✤ This is why I called it jealousy versus stupidity.

As long as we mentioned the veiling of women, we should understand that wearing the veil is only an order for Muslim free white women, but it's not the case for a slave woman.

Why Veiling Forced on women?

We know that Muslims always have their mouth full of preserving the rights of women, claiming that veiling is to protect them! And here's to show you from the Muslims own words how they themselves try to explain to us the issue of forcing the veil on women.

From an Islamic website islamicfaq.org/veil/index.html I quote:

Q1: What is the concept of veiling in Islam?

A: Islam stresses the relationship between body and mind. In covering the body, one shields the heart from impurities. Men are instructed to restrain or avert their eyes from women, and women are expected to wear loose outer garments and to cover their heads and bosoms.

The ultimate goal of veiling is righteousness of the heart.

The purpose of hijab (veiling) in Islam is primarily to inspire modesty in both men and women. Women are admonished in the Holy Qur'an to cover their heads and to pull their coverings over their bosoms. Men are instructed in the Holy Qur'an to lower their gazes.

In chapter 24, verse 32 Allah says: 'And say to the believing women that they restrain their eyes and guard their private parts, and they display not their beauty and embellishments except that which is apparent thereof, and that they draw their head-covers over their bosoms, and they display not their beauty or their embellishment thereof save to their husbands, or to their fathers, or the fathers of their husbands, or their sons, or the sons of their husbands, or their brothers or the sons of their brothers, or the sons of their sisters, or their women, or what their right hands possess, or such of male attendants who have no wickedness in them, or young chil-

dren who have not yet attained any concept of the private parts of women. And they walk not in a style that such of their beauty as they conceal is noticed. And turn you to Allah all together, O believers, that you may succeed.'

Usually I don't like to use nasty words when I speak, but I cannot withhold myself from saying that the real reason behind Hijab or veiling has nothing to do with the reason as presented to us by Muslims on that website. That is nothing but a total fabrication.

First of all the one who made the article to teach us about Islam does not know how to read the Qur'an because he quoted the number of the wrong verse, thinking the Qur'an is organized in the correct way, where in fact it is not. So in the Arabic Quran the verse number comes always at the end of the verse not before it.

- ✦ He fabricated the translation adding the fourth sentence **"and that they draw their head-covers"** which cannot be located anywhere in the Arabic Qur'an.
- ✦ So then why they added the head covering in the verse?
- ✦ Muslims generally speaking they are copy paste.
- ✦ They try to justify stupid behavior, by creating a stupid lie, hoping that nobody would find out, and if you find out who dares to question?

The ass of the prophet's wife Sauda was behind the veiling verses

If you remember in the previous page from the Muslims website they said that Allah ordered the women to cover their head but that cannot be found anywhere in the Qur'an. If we go back to the same chapter, translation made by them, in Qur'an 24:31 we read this false fabricated translation **"and that they draw their head-covers over their bosoms,"** in the Arabic text we will never find anywhere where it mentioned **"their head-covers"**

Qur'an 24 :32 Yusuf Ali translation: *And say to the believing women that they should lower their gaze and guard their modesty; that they should not display their beauty and ornaments except what (must ordinarily) appear thereof; that they should draw their veils over their bosoms and not display their beauty except to their husbands, their fathers, their husband's fathers, their sons, their husbands' sons, their brothers or their brothers' sons, or their sisters' sons, or their women, or the slaves whom their right hands possess, or male servants free of physical needs, or small children who have no sense of the shame of sex; and that they should not strike their feet in order to draw attention to their hidden ornaments. And O ye Believers! turn ye all together towards Allah, that ye may attain Bliss.*

As you see the head covering doesn't even exist not even in a single verse in the

Qur'an, and it was 'Umar Ibn Al-Khattab, making fun of Muhammad's wives and specifically the old one Sauda, forcing Muhammad to order his wives to veil themselves when they go out to defecate, and proof of that is just in the front of our eyes in the story reported by 'Aisha:

'Aisha narrated that the wives of Allah's Messenger used to go out in the cover of night when they went to open fields to do shit. 'Umar Ibn Al-Khattab used to say:Allah's Messenger, ask your ladies to observe veil, but Allah's Messenger did not do that. So there went out Sauda, daughter of Zarn'a, the wife of Allah's Messenger, throughout one of the evenings when it was dark. She was a tall statured lady. 'Umar called her saying: Sauda, we recognize you. (He did this with the hope that the verses pertaining to veil would be revealed.) 'Aisha said: Allah, the Exalted and Glorious, then revealed the verses pertaining to veil. Sahih Muslim 2170 d, Sahih al-Bukhari 146

And actually, this story raised many questions in my mind:

- ✤ It was 'Umar Ibn Al-Khattab the person who kept asking Muhammad to force his women to veil themselves.
- ✤ It was Muhammad repeatedly ignoring that request and refusing it!
- ✤ 'Umar Ibn Al-Khattab he has a plan to chase the wives of Muhammad while their butt is exposed and harassed them by saying "'Umar called her saying: Sauda, we recognize you."
- ✤ He is watching the naked Women, observing and shouting, proud of himself and not worried of the husband getting angry!
- ✤ What do you think if you have a friend and you live in the old days where people don't have a bathroom, and this friend comes to your house looking at your wife while she is following the call of nature, and he screams saying "we recognized you"
- ✤ And then in a mysterious way Allah sent his verse ordering the wives of the prophet to cover their ass and their breast!
- ✤ In fact 'Umar later he was bragging about that Allah agreed with him in many things and one of them is women veiling!

'Umar the prophet's companions makes Qur'an; Reported *'Umar (bin Al-Khattab): My Lord agreed with me in three things: 1. I said,"O Allah's Apostle, I wish we took the place of Abraham as our praying place (for some of our prayers). So came the Divine revelation And take you (people) the station of Abraham as a place of prayer (for some of your prayers e.g. two Rakat of Tawaf of Ka'ba)". (2.125) 2. And as regards the (verse of) the veiling of the women, I said, 'O Al-*

lah's Apostle! I wish you ordered your wives to veil themselves from the men because good and bad ones talk to them.' So the verse of the veiling of the women was revealed. 3. Once the wives of the Prophet made a united front against the Prophet and I said to them, 'It may be if he (the Prophet) divorced you, (all) that his Lord (Allah) will give him instead of you wives better than you.' So these verses the same as I had said was revealed." (66.5). (Bukhari, Book #8, Hadith #395)

From the story above it's clear that the Qur'an is made by Muhammad as a copy of 'Umar, wherein we find major laws affecting Muslims' beliefs;

- Directions of the prayer to Mecca instead of to Jerusalem.
- To cover women, to wear Hijab and veil.
- Involving in a very private matter regarding women's obedience to Muhammad.

And God knows how many more verses were made by 'Umar or others, that we do not know about, because we can only examine a history written and made by Muslims, and as you know no one would like to witness against himself, so why Muslims would! However what we have was hard to hide, for it's even showing in the Qur'an, where it gives us more details about people in Muhammad's time that accused him of forgery and copying others as we read in Qur'an; 25:4 *"And those who Kufar(disbelievers) say: This is nothing but a lie which he has forged, and other people have assisted him at it; so indeed they have done injustice and spoke a falsehood."*

And more news of copying shows up in Qur'an 16:103 "And indeed We know (Allah talking) that they (The Arab people of Mecca) say: **"It is only a human being who teaches him"**

To be killed for getting married if you are a slave!

Islam encourages people to get married, but while getting married is a free choice for the free white people, what if you are a slave?

The Prophet said: If any slave marries without the permission of his masters, he is a fornicator. Sunan Abi Dawud 2078

Imagine you would be punished severely for getting married without the permission from the master who owns you, and what is the crime? You got married!

Obviously, the slave's slavery goes way beyond doing a service to the master, who is in full control even in your personal and sexual life, additional to all of this you are not allowed even to choose your friends without permission from your master, or even after you are freed from slavery you will always be the slave of the choices of your previous master.

Allah's Messenger said: *He who takes anyone as his ally without the consent of his previous master, there will be the curse of Allah and His angels upon him (the free to slave), and neither, any obligatory act of his nor the supererogatory one will be accepted by Allah.* Sahih Muslim 1508 a

Hijab is for free white women not the slave one

There's thousands of articles and videos made by Muslims to convince the Africans that Islam treats all humans equally, and that Islam works hard in that direction, but the truth is outright the opposite, Islamic history books written by the hands of Muslims and accepted by them expose the lies and the falsehood of the deceitful Islamic propaganda.

A slave women entered upon 'Umar IbnAl-Khatab, he recognized her(as a slave), therefore he said to her are you free from slavery now? She said: no.

Therefore, he said so why are you covering your head? The cover is for the free women from the wives of the believers take it off, I should not do that immediately therefore he lashed her on her head until she took it off. Al-Mu'anaf volume 2 Page 134

حدثنا علي بن مسهر عن المختار بن فلفل عن أنس بن مالك قال : دخلت على عمر بن الخطاب أمة قد كان يعرفها لبعض المهاجرين أو الأنصار وعليها جلباب متقنعة به فسألها عتقت قالت : لا قال : فما بال الجلباب ضعيه عن رأسك إنما الجلباب على الحرائر من نساء المؤمنين فتلكأت فقام إليها بالدرة فضرب بها برأسها حتى ألقته عن رأسها

In fact, the caliph 'Umar not only forced slave women to uncover their head but he also forced them to be topless in his house all the time even while serving his guests.

It was reported by 'Hammad bin Salamah he said: the female slaves of 'Umar use to serve us exposing their hair, and their breast are free shaking(when they walk) and exposing the bracelets in their legs. Tafsir Yhya Ibn Salam volume 1 Page 441.

وقد رواه يحيى بن سلام في تفسيره (1/ 144) : حَدَّثَنِي حَمَّادٌ وَنَصْرُ بْنُ طَرِيفٍ، عَنْ ثُمَامَةَ بْنِ أَنَس

بْنِ مَالِكٍ ، عَنْ أَنَسِ بْنِ مَالِكٍ قَالَ: « كُنَّ جَوَارِي عُمَرَ يَخْدُمْنَنَا كَاشِفَاتِ الرُّءُوس، تَضْطَرِبُ ثُدِيُّهُنَّ بَادِيَةٌ خِدَامُهُنَّ "

And it is so clear that even the Qur'an gives an additional reason why the free women should dress differently, so when walking on the road the Muslims would recognize them as free Muslim women and she would not be a raped or sexually assaulted, and again I'm going to use the Muhammadans' translation to avoid the Muslims' games claiming I provided false translations:

Qur'an 33:59 Yusuf Ali's translation: *O Prophet! Tell thy wives and daughters, and the believing women, that they should cast their outer garments over their persons (when abroad): that is most convenient, that they should be known (as such) and not molested. And Allah is Oft-Forgiving, Most Merciful.*

Muhsin Khan's translation: *Qur'an 33:59 O Prophet! Tell your wives and your daughters and the women of the believers to draw their cloaks (veils) all over their bodies (i.e. screen themselves completely except the eyes or one eye to see the way). That will be better, that they should be known (as free respectable women) so as not to be annoyed. And Allah is Ever Oft-Forgiving, Most Merciful.*

So, we can say with no mistake, that the Islamic Society allowed Muslims to harass and assault sexually any woman that is not a free woman, and in order to avoid confusion between the free women and the slave women, so Allah aka Muhammad enforced two kinds of clothing, the veil for the free white Muslim women and revealing clothing for the slave one.

Which means the purpose of all of this has nothing to do with preventing men from temptation but is solely to prevent savage society from molesting or sexually assaulting free women, however there is no issue if you do that to slave women you find in your way.

The Prophet raised his hand to beat her for refusing sex

We went out with the Prophet (Allah pray on him and salute him) to a fenced property called Al-Shaut until we how arrived to point where this is two walls which we sat down. The Prophet (Allah pray on him and salute him) said, "sit down here," and went in (inside the property). The Jauniya (the name of the lady) had been brought and roomed in a house in a date-palm garden in the home of Umaima bint Al- Nu`man bin Shara'hil, and her wet-nurses was with her. When the Prophet (Allah pray on him and salute him) entered upon her, *he said to her, "Give me yourself (for sex) as a gift." She said, "how it is possible that a Queen would give herself to a Savage man?" The Prophet (Allah pray on him and salute him) raised his hand to slap her so that she might obey and do his request. She said, "I seek refuge with Allah from you." He said, "You have sought refuge with One Who gives refuge. Then the Prophet (Allah pray on him and salute him) came out to us and said, "O Abu Usaid! Give her two white linen dresses to wear and let her go back to her family." Sahih al-Bukhari 5255*

This story exposes some of the savage sexual behavior of Muhammad:

- ↵ What kind of man enters upon the house of a strange woman and asks her to take off her panty for him?
- ↵ The prophet never did beat women!
- ↵ Women never been forced into sex!
- ↵ Muslim women are respected and they are not a sex object!
- ↵ Muhammad was a very well-respected man as they claimed, but yet this man is asking a woman he never meet before to sleep with him as a gift!
- ↵ Very short conversation straight to the point, he entered up on her asking her for sexual intercourse, sounds like a horny horse, every time is a good time for it even if his friends are waiting outside!
- ↵ This woman not only refused to sleep with him but she called him savage.
- ↵ You can imagine how brave this woman to say what she said in the face of the first top leader of ISIS.
- ↵ Now we need to remember that this story as it is written by Muslims might not necessarily be the true story.
- ↵ To make it simple this is a story after filtration.
- ↵ If this is what the Muhammadans themselves are reporting to us, so I wonder what if we ask that to women whom he wanted to sleep with about her side of the story?

فَلَمَّا دَخَلَ عَلَيْهَا النَّبِيُّ صلى الله عليه وسلم قَالَ « هَبِي نَفْسَكِ لِي ". قَالَتْ وَهَلْ تَهَبُ الْمَلِكَةُ نَفْسَهَا لِلسُّوقَةِ .
قَالَ فَأَهْوَى بِيَدِهِ يَضَعُ يَدَهُ عَلَيْهَا لِتَسْكُنَ فَقَالَتْ أَعُوذُ بِاللَّهِ مِنْكَ

Split 80-year-old woman in two parts alive & raped her daughter

There is a woman her name is 'Um Qirfa she was over eighty years old and a highly respected woman between the Arab. She refused to acknowledge Muhammad to be a prophet and made poetry against him, so look what he did:

And the capture 'Um Qirfa and her name is Fatima daughter of Zam'aa son of Mas'adah , and he captured too her daughter with Abdulah Ibn Mas'adah, and he(Muhammad) ordered Ibn Mas'ada to slaughter her so he tide her legs into two camels and ran them in opposite directions of each other so he split her into two pieces and then they brought in the front of him(Muhammad) the daughter of 'um Qirfa and Abdulah Ibn Mas'adah, and the daughter of 'um Qirfa from the shares of Salamah Ibn Al-Akwa'a because it was him who captured her, and she was from a very honorable family between her people, and the Arab use to say who is more honorable then 'Um Qirfa? therefore the prophet he ask him to give her to him and she was given to him!

Sirah Ibn Hisham Al-'Hameri volume 4 Page 1035. Book of Al Magazi wal Al-Saeer, the attack of Zaid Ibn Harithah in the valley of Qura. Book of Tarikh Al-'Tabari volume 5 book Tarikh Al-'Umam wal Mulook 2/127

وأسر أم قرفة وهي فاطمة بنت زمعة بن بدر وكانت عند حذيفة بن بدر عجوزاً كبيرة وبنت لها وعبد الله ابن مسعدة فأمر زيد بن حارثة أن تقتل أم قرفة فقتلها قتلاً عنيفاً وربط برجليها حبلين ثم ربطا إلى بعيرين شتى حتى شقاها. ثم قدموا على رسول الله صلّى الله عليه وسلّم بابنة أم قرفة وبعبد الله بن مسعدة فكانت بنت أم قرفة لسلمة بن الأكوع كان هو الذي أصابها وكانت في بيت شرف من قومها. كانت العرب تقول لو كنت أعز من أم قرفة فسألها رسول الله صلّى الله عليه وسلّم فوهبها له
الكتاب: عيون الأثر في المغازي والسير ـ سرية زيد بن حارثة إلى وادي القرى
الكاتب: ابن سيد الناس

Conclusion:

- ↩ All the stories we heard before by the propaganda of the Muhammadans have nothing to do with the truth.
- ↩ The claim that Muhammad never killed women was nothing but a lie.
- ↩ A very old women but not old enough for him to let her go, instead he punished her for making a statement against him, by killing her in a very ugly, disgusting way.
- ↩ There is a video made by the Islamic State which is known as ISIS, where they tied a man between two tanks and tore him in two pieces exactly as their prophet did.
- ↩ As usual when Muhammad hears that there is someone very pretty, she simply has to end up in his bed, and this is exactly what he did with the daughter of 'Um Qirfa, and Safia and a long list of other women, killing their family in the morning, raping their daughters an hour after.

Muhammad's sexual illness or brain disorder

All the references in the stories mentioned by Muslims proved to us that he was suffering from a sexual illness, however I think it is a result of mental illness, so let us go together and read some of those stories: Muhammad the weakest person in the bedroom between all of mankind.

كنت من أقل الناس في الجماع حتى أنزل الله علي الكفيت، فما أريده من ساعة إلا وجدته ، وهو قدر
(فيها لحم

"I was the weakest person in sex between all of mankind until Allah sent to me a dish made of Al-kufet(kebab), and each time I requested Allah send it immediately, and it is a dish of meat!" Book Al 'Tabaqat Al-Kubra 10231

In the same page from the same book we quote: *"the Angel Gabriel he delivered to me a dish after I ate it I get the sexual power over 40 men"* Al Khasa's Al-Kubra by Imam Al-'Su'ty, V.1 page 119

قال رسول الله صلى الله عليه وسلم لقيني جبريل بقدر فأكلت منها وأعطيت الكفيت قوة أربعين رجلا
في الجماع

in the same book and page, we find this hadith: *"narrated by Ibn 'Umar that the prophet said Gabriel came to me with shish kebab dish, and I ate it therefore I got the Power of 40 man in Fucking and killing with no mercy"*

وأخرج عن ابن عمرو عن النبي {صلى الله عليه وسلم} قال أعطيت قوة أربعين رجلا في البطش
والنكاح

And the question should be:

↬ why is Muhammad mentioning that he was the weakest person between all mankind if he is not?

↬ What is the purpose or the real reason for him to mention such a private confession that he was the weakest person between all mankind?

↬ Don't we learn from this story that Allah cares very much for Muhammad's private part power, and no way he will not give him the help that he needs?

↬ However the Quran mentioned that if Allah wanted something to happen he just said 'be' and it is going to be. So why didn't he say 'be' in order to fix the sexual problem of the poor prophet, whose penis is not functioning at all?

"(Allah) The Magnificent Originator of the heavens and the earth, and when He decrees an matter, He only says to it, Be, so there it is." Quran 2:117.

And the last thing I want to say is, as long as the story is mentioning the god of Muhammad sending him a dish of shish kebab in order to fix the sexual problem, does this mean that not all sorts of shish kebab would fix sexual problems? Or maybe only Allah knows (best) the mysterious recipes for sexual enhancee ment! And one more question, this dish of shish kebab, was it halal beef or pork? Hot or cold?

Final conclusion, no god can make shish kebab like Allah!

And that explains why the Quran is stating the following: *"Will ye call upon Baal and forsake the Best of Creators"* Quran 36:125.

If I'm the prophet I will make a new verse similar to this verse but I will change one word, I will replace the best of the creators, with the best of cookers! And don't forget to ask yourself how the god of Islam brags about being the best of the creators, but yet the Muslims do claim that he is the only creator, therefore is he the best between none??

Going back to the story, Muhammad being the weakest person in sexuality, as I believe the reason for him to say such a thing was because he was exposed with his illness.

In the time of Muhammad, remember he used to live in a small village and everyone knows everyone. The fact is, it is a tribe and all are one family, news spreading faster than the internet and technology nowadays, and it is obvious that the women which slept with Muhammad, had a problem with him and they did talk about it. From my experience as a person who came from the Middle East I know how strict our culture is, and no man whatsoever would like to mention that he is suffering from a sexual weakness, for that is considered as shameful, in fact until today it's extremely embarrassing for the man.

And for sure I'm speaking about the cultural view, because in my opinion there is no shame in any kind of illness, and besides that it is not your choice to be suffering from an illness.

And therefore, we see that the Muslims today in their books, keep mentioning stories about how powerful the prophet was in sex, because of their culture sexuality is the only proof that you are the macho man.

"It was reported by 'Taous and his father that the prophet was given the sexual power of 40 man" Al Khasa's Al-Kubra by Imam Al-'Su'ty, V.1 page 119.

الكتاب : الخصائص الكبرى
المؤلف / أبو الفضل جلال الدين عبد الرحمن أبي بكر السيوطي
أخبرنا محمد بن عمر عن معمر عن بن طاوس عن أبيه قال أعطي رسول الله صلى الله عليه وسلم قوة
أربعين رجلا في الجماع

And why and how the Muslims trusted the statement of Muhammad that he was given the power of 40 men, and shouldn't we ask ourselves what equals the sexual power of 40 men?

↬ First, how Muhammad could calculate his ability and measurement of his sexuality to be equal to 40 men?

↬ Why it's not 41 or 39 ? Are 40 men enough to satisfy the needs of the horny prophet?

↬ Why did Allah send the dish to increase his sexuality 40 times only, why not 400 times?

↬ Does this mean that Muhammad used to do it at least 40 times a day?

↬ If we divide 40 times by 16 hours given we stay awake a day that means Muhammad should have sex almost 3 times every single hour.

↬ Should I believe that Muhammad is a prophet because he had such sexual potency?

↬ Was Muhammad unqualified or fit to be a prophet when he said:

"I was the weakest person in sex between all of mankind until Allah sent to me a dish made of Al-kufet(kebab)"?

In the book of hadith, we read this: *"The believer shall be given in paradise such and such strength in F*** (intercourse)."* it was said: *"O Messenger of Allah! And will he be able to do that?"* He said: *"He will be given the strength of a hundred."* Jami` at-Tirmidhi Vol. 4, Book 12, Hadith 2536

↬ Based on the promise the prophet of Islam made to his men, as long as he got the power of 40 men on earth and Allah would make each believer able to do it a 100 times, does that mean Muhammad's sexual power would be 40 times the 100?

40 x 100 = 4000 men

But it's not only me who comes with this number, Muslims agreed: *From the narration of Zaid Ibn Ar'qam Raf'ah he said: "each man in the heaven of Allah would have the power of 100 men, to eat to drink, sexual intercourse, and sex desire, therefore based on this calculation, our prophet would have the power of 4000(in all of those things)."* Fath al-Bari fi Sharh Sahih al-Bukhari, Book of cleaning(Gusil) page 450

من حديث زيد بن أرقم رفعه " إن الرجل من أهل الجنة ليعطى قوة مائة في الأكل والشرب والجماع والشهوة " فعلى هذا يكون حساب قوة نبينا أربعة آلاف .

On top of that, we will see that later on, it doesn't stop by Muslims praising the sexuality of their prophet, they glorify his feces also.

The sex Hero champion Muhammad

Anas bin Malik said, "The Prophet used to do all his wives in a round, during part of an hour and they were eleven in number." I asked Anas, "Had the Prophet the strength for it?" Anas replied, "We used to say that the Prophet) was given the strength of thirty (men)." Sahih al-Bukhari 268

In the Muslims' translation they replaced the word Sa'a with "during the day and night" but in fact it's nothing but a lie, the word Sa'a in Arabic today is used as a word meaning an hour, but it means in the time of Muhammad not more than 20 minutes, but because the translator felt how awkward this story is and how no one would believe such a stupid thing that there is a man that can have sex with 11 women in 20 minutes, it's mad and a clear lie, regardless of the ability of a man to do so or not.

Because if we divide the time over 11 women we got less than 2 minutes for each woman to have sex with! Even a rabbit needs more time to finish it.

- Was he doing group sex so he does not need time to go from house to house because it takes place all in one bed?
- Were all having their period in the same day!
- 11 wives with one man in 20 minutes, who does the counting, how do they know?
- The one who reported the story is a man called "Anas bin Malik" how he was able to find out such a thing?
- Muhammad used to tell his sexual adventures to his men?
- The answer based on all previous references is yes.
- But is it not Muhammad who said that only wicked men do so?

Abu Sa'id al-Khudri reported that Allah's Messenger said: *The most wicked among the people in the eye of Allah on the Day of judgment is the man who does his wife (sexual intercourse) and she does him (sexual intercourse), and then he reveals her secret.* Sahih Muslim 1437 a

The miracle of feces and the urine

Because the prophet Muhammad cannot be like any of us, so Allah was watching carefully to take care of his urine and feces.

"Narrated by Jaber if the prophet made me ride behind him, in my mouth was the seal (the prophet's mole) and he smells like Musk, he wanted to defecate and the ground opens and swallow his feces and his piss, immediately and right after very nice smell produced" Al-Shifa bta'reef Hokok Al-Mustafa page 154

كتاب الشفا بتعريف حقوق المصطفى: 451] [وروى المزني : عن جابر : أردفني النبي - صلى]
الله عليه وسلم - خلفه ، فالتقمت خاتم النبوة بفمي ، فكان ينم علي مسكا] ، وقد حكى بعض المعتنين
بأخباره ، وشمائله ، وثمانله - صلى الله عليه وسلم - أنه كان إذا أراد أن يتغوط انشقت الأرض فابتلعت غائطه ،
وبوله ، وفاحت لذلك رائحة طيبة - صلى الله عليه وسلم

I was thinking about the real reason that Allah is immediately hiding the prophet's urine and feces, by making the earth instantly swallow whatever he dumps, I could not find the answer except it must be a National security matter!

If you're a Muslim who can give us the real reason behind this story I mean sorry " the miracle" please don't hesitate to inform us, especially about the feces, fart, and Allah who is making it perfume!

The Muslims claim that they don't worship Muhammad, yet they're fabricating tons of stories, to the point not only they do praise him, but they praise his fart and feces, additional to his urine.

In fact tons of stories just to praise his private parts, his smell, his sweat. In my previous book The Deception of Allah, you can read how they fight over the left over water from washing his underwear, and about Muslims washing their faces with it.

And things went even more crazy to the point they were drinking his urine: "It was narrated from the Sahih (trustworthy) Hadith, that the prophet he used to have a container to urinate in it and he use to leave it under his bed,... so he did urinate in it at night, and he left the container under the bed, and when he grabbed it again he found the container empty from his urine, so he questioned a woman her name is Barakah, the servant of 'Um Habiba (one of Muhammad wives) the one she came with her from Ethiopia, where is the my urine it was in this container, she said I drunk it Messenger Allah" Sunan Al-Nusa'i, book of pure, volume 1 page 32

وَخَرَّجَ حَدِيثَهَا فِي صَحِيحِهِ (قَالَتْ : كَانَ لِلنَّبِيِّ صَلَّى اللهُ عَلَيْهِ وَسَلَّمَ قَدَحٌ مِنْ عِيْدَانٍ يَبُولُ فِيهِ وَيَضَعُهُ
تَحْتَ السَّرِيرِ) هَذَا مُخْتَصَرٌ ، وَقَدْ أَتَمَهُ ابْنُ عَبْدِ الْبَرِ فِي الِاسْتِيعَابِ فَقَالَ : فَبَالَ لَيْلَةً فَوَضَعَ تَحْتَ سَرِيرِهِ
، فَجَاءَ فَإِذَا الْقَدَحُ لَيْسَ فِيهِ شَيْءٌ ، فَسَأَلَ الْمَرْأَةَ يُقَالُ لَهَا بَرَكَةُ كَانَتْ [ص: 23] تَخْدُمُ أُمَّ حَبِيبَةَ جَاءَتْ
مَعَهَا مِنَ الْحَبَشَةِ فَقَالَ : أَيْنَ الْبَوْلُ الَّذِي كَانَ فِي هَذَا الْقَدَحِ؟ فَقَالَتْ : شَرِبْتُهُ يَا رَسُولَ اللَّهِ

If you see my private part you go blind!

And things get even more crazy and out of hands, where Muhammad claimed, that if somebody would look at his penis or his anus he should go blind immediately, I wonder why, maybe it is so shiny!

And how do his wives have sex with him? They used to wear electric welding masks?

Narrated by 'Aisha she said: *"I never ever saw the private part of Allah Messenger"*, and narrated by 'Ali: the prophet said: *"No one should wash my private part except me, because if any saw my private parts he will go blind"* Al-Shifa bta'reef Hokok Al-Mustafa, volume 1, page 156

وعن عائشة - رضي الله عنها - : [ما رأيت فرج رسول الله - صلى الله عليه وسلم - قط] ، وعن علي - رضي الله عنه - : أوصاني النبي - صلى الله عليه وسلم - لا يغسله غيري ، فإنه لا يرى أحد عورتي إلا طمست عيناه

And actually I ask myself this very simple question, if the statement of his wife 'Aisha is correct, that means she never ever saw Muhammad's private part, and he did scare her from looking at it, otherwise she will go blind as a punishment from Allah, for sure none of us believes this made up excuse of Muhammad that if his wife should look, she will go blind, then what is the reason he doesn't want his wives to look at him naked?

It's not my nature to go low and speak about private part, however for the benefit of learning I got to ask a few questions based on the previous story:

Muhammad doesn't want them to see his private part for one of the following reasons:

- He had a birth defect on his private part, which he's trying to hide.
- It was so small and he was afraid that you might see it for that reason.
- And most likely he was suffering from birth defects, which explains why he used to urinate always seated as a woman.

Narrated 'Aisha: *"Whoever tells you that the Messenger of Allah urinated standing up, do not believe him, for he never urinate except while squatting."* Sunan an-Nasa'i Vol. 1, Book 1, Hadith 29

It might come to your mind, that maybe he used to urinate because it was the custom of the Arab?

44

We find the answer in this story: *Sufian Al-Thawri said: regarding the Hadith of 'Aisha- 'I saw him always urinating while sitting down', he said: a man he knows more about that (the urine of Muhammad) than she do.' Ahmad bin 'Abd Al-Rahman said: 'It was the custom of the Arabs to urinate standing up. Do you not see that in the Hadith of 'Abd Al-Rahman bin 'Hasanah it was said: 'He sits down to urinate as a woman does.'"* Sunan Ibn Majah Vol. 1, Book 1, Hadith 309.

The devil controlling my sexdrive

I'm trying very hard to keep this book small, but yet rich with information, and I think it might be very useful for you, in case you have any sexual problem to learn from what happened to the prophet, you never know what might happen to you too!

Narrated 'Aisha: (Muhammad's child-wife): *"The Prophet continued for such-and-such period imagining that he had slept (had sexual intercourse) with his wives, when in fact he had not. One day he said to me, 'O 'Aisha! Allah has enlightened me regarding a matter about which I had asked Him. There came to me two men, one of them drew near my feet and the other near my head. The one near my feet asked the one near my head, 'What is wrong with this man?' (asking about Muhammad). The second man replied, 'He is under the effect of black magic'. The first man asked, 'Who activated magic on him?' The other replied, 'Lubaid Ibn Al-'Asam'. The first man asked, 'What substance did he use?' The other responded, 'The strip of the pollen of a male date tree with a comb and the hair stuck to it, kept under a stone in the well of Zarwan'. Then the Prophet went to that well and said, 'This is the same well which was shown to me. The tops of its date-palm trees look like the heads of the devils and its water looks like the Henna extract'. Afterwards the Prophet commanded that those things be taken out. I said, 'O Allah's Apostle! Won't you expose the magic object?' The Prophet replied, 'Allah has healed me and I hate to circulate the evil among the people'. 'Aisha added, 'The magician Lubaid ibn Al-'Asam was a man from the tribe of Zuraiq, an ally of the Jews.* Sahih al-Bukhari 6063

صحيح البخاري » كتاب الأدب » باب قول الله تعالى إن الله يأمر بالعدل والإحسان وإيتاء ذي القربى
باب قول الله تعالى إن الله يأمر بالعدل والإحسان وإيتاء ذي القربى وينهى عن الفحشاء والمنكر والبغي
يعظكم لعلكم تذكرون وقوله إنما بغيكم على أنفسكم ثم بغي عليه لينصرنه الله وترك إثارة الشر على
مسلم أو كافر
حدثنا الحميدي حدثنا سفيان حدثنا هشام بن عروة عن أبيه عن عائشة رضي الله عنها قالت 5716
مكث النبي صلى الله عليه وسلم كذا وكذا يخيل إليه أنه يأتي أهله ولا يأتي قالت عائشة فقال لي ذات
يوم يا عائشة إن الله أفتاني في أمر استفتيته فيه أتاني رجلان فجلس أحدهما عند رجلي والآخر عند

رأسي فقال الذي عند رجلي للذي عند رأسي ما بال الرجل قال مطبوب قال ومن طبه
قال لبيد بن أعصم قال وفيم قال في جف طلعة ذكر في مشط ومشاقة تحت رعوفة في بئر ذروان
فجاء النبي صلى الله عليه وسلم فقال هذه البئر التي أريتها كأن رءوس نخلها رءوس الشياطين وكأن
ماءها نقاعة الحناء فأمر به النبي صلى الله عليه وسلم فأخرج قالت عائشة فقلت يا رسول الله فهلا تعني
تنشرت فقال النبي صلى الله عليه وسلم أما الله فقد شفاني وأما أنا فأكره أن أثير على الناس شرا قالت
ولبيد بن أعصم رجل من بني زريق حليف ليهود

- ↭ Notice with me here that the reason that the Prophet of Islam imagined himself having sexual intercourse with his wives is due to the black magic.
- ↭ When a man imagined such a thing to the point he could not recognize if it was a sexual relationship or just imagination, how bad his situation was?
- ↭ None of us believe in black magic anyway, so what is a scientific explanation for this?

I am sure you heard of very well-known illnesses called epilepsy and schizophrenia and they both share many symptoms:

From the National health institute we quote: *"Hallucinations are sensory experiences that occur in the absence of a stimulus. These can occur in any of the five senses (vision, hearing, smell, taste, or touch). "Voices" (auditory hallucinations) are the most common type of hallucination in schizophrenia. Many people with the disorder hear voices. The voices can either be internal, seeming to come from within one's own mind, or they can be external, in which case they can seem to be as real as another person speaking. The voices may talk to the person about his or her behavior, command the person to do things, or warn the person of danger. Sometimes the voices talk to each other, and sometimes people with schizophrenia talk to the voices that they hear. People with schizophrenia may hear voices for a long time before family and friends notice the problem…. Suicidal thoughts and behaviors are very common among people with schizophrenia"*

And most likely he was infected by this illness since his childhood.

Epilepsy of Muhammad

We have some stories reported by Muslims about some incidents that happened to Muhammad while he was under the age of five years old, as we read:

Anas b. Malik declared that Gabriel came to the Messenger of Allah while he was playing with his playmates. He took grasp of him and lay him horizontal to the ground and ripped open his chest and took out the heart from it and after that extracted a blood-clot out of it and said: "That was the part of Satan in thee. And afterwards he washed it with the water of Zamzam in a golden bowl and then it was stitched together and restored to its place. The boys came running toward his mother, i. e. his nurse, and said: Verily, Muhammad has been murdered. They all rushed toward him (and found him all right) His color was changed, Anas said. I saw the marks of the needle on his chest." Sahih Muslim 162 c.

From the story we learn that he was playing with his playmates and then suffered from an epileptic seizure. That is certain, the rest of the story is nothing but fiction made by Muhammad later.

If you notice with me in the story at this time as a child he was not living with his parents but with a nurse, a Bedouin woman hired by his family to take care of him. Which I find rather weird and strange because why a family of a child and his mother would hand out a child to a stranger who has no address and God knows where you will end up!

Obviously, his family did notice that he was suffering from a problem and therefore decided to send him away in an attempt to get rid of him, however his Bedouin nurse sent him back to his family, after this incident occurred because she was worried he might not live. If what happened to him would happen again while being under her supervision then she would responsible for his death.

Then we see Muhammad saying the same story about an angel cutting his chest and installing the dish of wisdom and faith while he is an adult.

But this time the hallucination happened to him while he was in Mecca as a man and a "prophet", not as a child where we notice that Muhammad got a lot more worse and that is normal as the illness becomes more complex, and the hallucinating becomes so strong which is caused by schizophrenia.

Anas b. Malik reported by the authority of Malik b. Sa' sa'a, that the Prophet of Allah said: *I was near the House (i. e. Ka'baa) in a state between sleep and wakefulness when I heard someone say: He is the third among the two persons. Then he came to me and took me with him. Then a golden basin containing the water of Zamzam (spring of water in Mecca) was brought to me and my chest was opened to such and such location. Qatada said: I asked him (I e. the narrator) who was with me. and what he meant by such and such (part). He the narrator replied: he meant that it was opened to the lower part of his belly (Then the narrator continues reporting what Muhammad said): My heart was extracted and it was washed by the water of Zamzam and then it was returned in its original location after which it was filled with faith and wisdom. I was then brought a white beast who is called al-Buraq, bigger than a donkey and smaller than a mule. Its stride was as far as far as Horizon. I was risen on it, and then we went forth until we reached the lowest sky Gabriel asked for the (gate) to be opened, and it was said: Who is he? He replied: Gabriel. It was again said: Who is with thee? He replied: Muhammad. It was said: Has he been requested to come? He (Gabriel) said: Yes. He (the Prophet) said: Then (the gate) was opened for us (, and it was said): Welcome unto him! His arrival is an honor. Then we came to Adam (peace be upon him). And he (the narrator) narrated the whole account of the hadith. (The Holy Prophet) Saw that he met Jesus in the second heaven, John the Baptist in the third heaven, Yusuf in the third, Idris in the fourth. Aaron in the fifth, then we traveled on until we reached the sixth heaven and came to Moses, and I greeted him, and he said: Welcome unto bias brother and bias prophet. And when I passed (by him) he wept, and a voice was heard saying: What makes thee weep? He said: My Lord, he is a young man whom thou hast sent after me (as a prophet) and his followers will enter Paradise in greater numbers than my followers. Then we traveled on until we reached the seventh heaven, and I came to Ibrahim. He the commentator narrated in this hadith that the Prophet of Allah described that he saw four rivers, which flowed from (the root of the Lote-tree of the farthest limits): two manifest rivers and two hidden rivers. I said: ' Gabriel! What are these rivers? He replied: The two hidden rivers are the rivers of Paradise, and about the two manifest ones, they are the Nile and the Euphrates. Then the built House was raised up to me. I said: O Gabriel! what is this? He replied: It is the Bait-Al-Ma'mur. Seventy thousand angels enter it daily and after they come out, they never will return. Two containers were then brought to me. The first one held in wine and the second one held in milk, and both were placed before me. I selected milk. It was said: You did lawful Allah will guide rightly through you your nation on the natural course. afterwards fifty prayers daily were made obligatory for me. And after that he narrated the rest of the hadith to the end.* Sahih Muslim 164 a

As we notice here, the same story was mentioned, the chest of Muhammad being cut open when he was a child, and happening again to Muhammad when he was an adult man, with the exact same details as a start;

- Chest operation.
- Washing his heart with the water of Zamzam
- Installing a dish faith and wisdom! (I wish I can get a dish of knowledge too, that would have saved me 20 years of my life studying Islam!)
- Seeing various prophets in several heavens, but according to Islam only Jesus

is alive in heaven and the rest is dead! As we read: *"And in no way, is Muhammad (anything) except a Messenger;* **the Messengers have already passed away before him.** *Then, will it be that, in case he dies or is killed, will you turn (Literally: turn (s) over on) on your heels? And whoever turns (Literally: turn (s) over on) on his heels, then he will never harm Allah in anything; and Allah will recompense the thankful.* Quran 3:144 Dr. Muhammad Ghali Translation

This story is either because Muhammad was suffering from hallucinations, or it's just a pure fabrication of this man.

However, if we reconnect this story to the story we mentioned before, which is speaking of him imagining himself having sexual intercourse with his wives but in fact he never did that would lead us to a mental disorder.

The White Angel cloned by the Black devil!

We should make it a clear, that according to Islam the devil is black however in the coming story it looked like the devil was able to use a whitening product made by Victoria's Secret and was able to turn white, and if Michael Jackson can do it why Mr. Satan cannot?

Once there was a Muslim, making comments about my questioning why Islam insisted that the devil is black. This smart Abdul (Muslim) answered me by saying: "have you ever seen a black angel" I replied: have you ever seen a white one!

Obviously, Muhammad considered the black color as the color of the devil, and sometimes he exceeded his foolishness to the point he considered animals are the devil himself just because they are black:

Abu Zher reported: *The Messenger of 'Allah said: When any one of you stands for prayer be sure there is a thing before him equal to the back of the saddle that covers him and in case there is not before him (something) equal to the back of the saddle, his prayer would be not accepted if an ass, woman, and black Dog, cross by, I said: O Abu Zher, what feature is there in a black dog which distinguish it from the red dog and the yellow dog? He said: Oh, son of my brother, I asked the Messenger of Allah as you are asking me, and he said: The black dog is a devil.* Sahih Muslim 510 a

Now this story alone as reported to us from the mouth of Muhammad is enough to prove me two things:

1. Muhammad is a sick racist, to the point he thinks even animals are the devil just because of the black color!
2. He has a mental illness, for this is the belief of a mad men and someone suffering not only from believing in superstition fictions, but also he is not as stable in his thinking.

However in the coming story we will see that the devil, by the fabrication of Muhammad, can be white when he wants, and can be black when he wants.

The devil is black, that is the way he is according to Muhammad, however when Muhammad delivered the Satanic verses, in order to protect himself and to explain why he accepted those verses to be said by him even though they are coming from the devil the excuse was: what can I do, this time he did come to me as white so I trusted him!

The more we read about Muhammad's life stories, the more we are convinced that this man is suffering from mental illness.

Most of you will have heard about the book called the Satanic verses by the author sir Salman Rushdie, in this book he did not say anything except a little tiny story written and reported in the Qur'an and in every Islamic book of interpretation.

To make the story short, according to the Qur'an Muhammad had received satanic verses, and he acknowledged in those verses that it is a must to worship the three daughters of Allah, however there's some hidden details 99% of people do not know about, and I believe you will never find one single Islamic book written in English, or a translation from Arabic to English reporting what I am going to show you: Qur'an 22:52: *We Never sent a Messenger or a Prophet before you (Muhammad) but when he did recite the revelation or spoke, Satan threw falsehood in it. But Allah abolishes that whatever Satan throws in. Then Allah establishes His Revelations. And Allah is All-Knower, All-Wise.* Tafsir Al-Kaber by Abu Baker Al-Razi chapter 22:52 Page 47.

Reported by Ibn 'Abbas from 'A'ta that he said: " *there is a Satan his title is the white, he came to the prophet in the image of the angel Gabriel, and he gave him this speech, and he(Muhammad) did recited, afterward Gabriel peace upon him questioning him recite again the verses therefore when he reached to that statements, Gabriel said: I did not tell you that! The prophet Allah pray on him and salute him said: someone came to me in your image and he place it on my tongue!*

Afterwards Al-Razi, continued defending Muhammad against some Muslims' interpretations and he said: *Some ignorant said: that the prophet because he was so devoted to make people believe on his faith, he was the one who did add those verses in order to make the pagans join his religion(!) and later he retreated from that statement, then he changed his mind.*

However there is no Muslim who would like any of those two statements because the first one is proving that he was not able to distinguish between what is false from Satan and what is from the true angel and, and if we believe the second statement, that would lead us to the conclusion that the prophet betrayed the inspiration(of Allah). And both statements prove that the prophet became an apostate of Islam!

قال ابن عباس رضي الله عنهما في رواية عطاء : إن شيطانا يقال له الأبيض أتاه على صورة جبريل عليه السلام ، وألقى عليه هذه الكلمة فقرأها فلما سمع المشركون ذلك أعجبهم ، فجاء جبريل عليه السلام فاستعرضه فقرأها فلما بلغ إلى تلك الكلمة قال جبريل عليه السلام : أنا ما جئتك بهذه . قال رسول الله صلى الله عليه وسلم : إنه أتاني آت على صورتك فألقاها على لساني . الطريق الثاني : قال بعض الجهال : إنه عليه السلام لشدة حرصه على إيمان القوم أدخل هذه الكلمة من عند نفسه ثم رجع عنها ، وهذان القولان لا يرغب فيهما مسلم البتة ؛ لأن الأول يقتضي أنه عليه السلام ما كان يميز بين الملك المعصوم والشيطان الخبيث ، والثاني يقتضي أنه كان خائنا في الوحي ، وكل واحد منهما خروج عن الدين

- ↬ It is so clear as I always say, the books of interpretation which are made by Muslim scholars, were never meant to explain the Qur'an but merely to dem fend the Qur'an.
- ↬ If you read all the books written by Muslims about those Satanic verses you will notice immediately how much they are in chaos to explain what happened!
- ↬ Where there are many opinions and each one of those opinions is as far from the other as possible.
- ↬ Regardless if the Muslims agree or not with each other, in the Qur'an it is clear that Muhammad received Satanic verses.
- ↬ And the story of Satan coming in the image of an angel as the "white Gabriel" will not change the fact that it is Muhammad who is not that trustworthy, and that he is imagining things or fabricating things, to the point that even the Muslims themselves thought about it and I quote: *"Some ignorant said: that the prophet because he was so devoted to make people believe on his faith, he was the one who did add those verses in order to make the pagans join his religion and later he retreated from that statement then he changed his mind."*
- ↬ So regardless if the verses were Muhammad's fabrication, or it is a true story as he claimed that Satan came to him in the image of a white angel, both stories prove to us one of two things, that he is either:

↦ Crazy man suffering from delusion.

↦ Or a false prophet as Al-Razi said "And it would lead us to believe that the prophet he betrayed the inspiration (of Allah) and both of them is proving that the prophet became an apostate of Islam!"

The same story appears in many books written by very high, trustworthy Muslim scholars like Al-Qurtbi in his interpretation Page 77, but he added a few more details:

Reported by Ibn 'Abbas that he said: *"there is a Satan and He throw some words in his reading, he came in the image of the angel Gabriel, and he told the prophet to say those are the goddess of high their intercession (the daughters of Allah) is a must and pleasing (to Allah).*

وقد قال ابن عباس : إن شيطانا يقال له الأبيض كان قد أتى رسول الله - صلى الله عليه وسلم - في صورة جبريل - عليه السلام - وألقى في قراءة النبي - صلى الله عليه وسلم - : تلك الغرانيق العلا ، وأن شفاعتهن لترتجى .

And I would like to add more questions about the white Satan story:

↦ If Satan is capable of making Qur'an, as the verse in the Qur'an states 22:52, then how stupid it is to find in the Qur'an a challenge made by the Qur'an author Muhammad aka Allah, challenging mankind and Satan to make Qur'an like his? **Qur'an 17:88 Say: "If the whole of mankind and Jins were to come together to make the like of this Qur'an, they could not generate the like thereof, even if they backed up each other with help and support."**

↦ So nobody can make or create the Qur'an but yet Muhammad received Satanic verses and he did not even notice this was not the Qur'an?

↦ As long as the devil can come as an angel, and he did already come to Muhammad as an angel, what is our guarantee that the one which Muhammad always sees is not the same devil?

↦ What is the guarantee that the verse which Muhammad mentioned in chapter 22 verse 52, that Allah Will cancel any Satanic verses given by Satan that the same verse is made by Satan himself, to make those who didn't notice the falsehood of Muhammad relax and make them believe, that this Satan was able to penetrate the mouth of the prophet adding falsehood in his mouth but yet Allah is going to take them out so "don't worry be happy"?

Muhammad hears voices

'Amr ibn Shurahbil said: *"The Messenger of Allah, Allah pray on him and salute him, whenever he went out to defecate, used to hear someone calling him 'O Mu-hammad!' And whenever he heard this, he used to flee a way. Waraqah Ibn Nawfal advised the Prophet to remain in his place next time when the caller calls him so that he hears what he want to say. And so when he went out, he heard the calling: 'O Muhammad!' He said: 'Here I am! At your service!' The caller said: 'Say: I bear witness that there is no god but Allah and I bear witness that Muhammad is the Messenger of Allah'.* Book of Asbab el Nuzul hadith 17

حَدَّثَنَا أَبُو عُثْمَانَ سَعِيدُ بْنُ أَحْمَدَ بْنِ مُحَمَّدٍ الزَّاهِدُ ، أَخْبَرَنَا جَدِّي ، قَالَ : أَخْبَرَنَا أَبُو عَمْرٍو الْحِيرِيُّ إِبْرَاهِيمُ بْنُ الْحَارِثِ ،وَ عَلِيُّ بْنُ سَهْلِ بْنِ الْمُغِيرَةِ ، قَالَا : حَدَّثَنَا يَحْيَى بْنُ أَبِي بُكَيْرٍ حَدَّثَنَا إِسْرَائِيلُ ، عَنْ أَبِي إِسْحَاقَ ، عَنْ أَبِي مَيْسَرَةَ أَنَّ رَسُولَ اللَّهِ صَلَّى اللَّهُ عَلَيْهِ وَسَلَّمَ كَانَ إِذَا بَرَزَ سَمِعَ مُنَادِيًا يُنَادِيهِ : يَا مُحَمَّدُ ، فَإِذَا سَمِعَ الصَّوْتَ انْطَلَقَ هَارِبًا ، فَقَالَ لَهُ وَرَقَةُ بْنُ نَوْفَلٍ : إِذَا سَمِعْتَ النِّدَاءَ فَاثْبُتْ حَتَّى تَسْمَعَ مَا يَقُولُ لَكَ : قَالَ : فَلَمَّا بَرَزَ سَمِعَ النِّدَاءَ : يَا مُحَمَّدُ ، فَقَالَ : لَبَّيْكَ ، قَالَ : قُلْ : أَشْهَدُ أَنْ لَا إِلَهَ إِلَّا اللَّهَ ، وَأَشْهَدُ أَنَّ مُحَمَّدًا رَسُولُ اللَّهِ ، ثُمَّ قَالَ : قُلْ : الْحَمْدُ لِلَّهِ رَبَّ

Trees and stones greeting Muhammad with Al-Salam Alykom!

Imagine if you see a man walking the street or in the woods, and each time he sees a rock he would hear rocks and trees speaking to him saying shalom!!!

Isn't this enough to prove that he is a mental person?

And each time the prophet go out to answer the call of nature, he used to lift up his clothing and go between the bushes, the bottom of the Valley in Mecca and he keeps looking left and right, and he would never pass by a rock or tree without it saying to him Salam Alykum.(peace to you)! And he keep doing that to hear as much Allah wanted him to hear. Ibn Kathir Al Bidaya Wal Nihaya volume 3, page 17.

اذا خرج لحاجة أبعد حتى يحسر الثوب عنه ويفضي الى شعاب مكة وبطون أوديتها فلا يمر بحجر ولا شجر إلا قال السلام عليك يا رسول الله قال فيلتفت حوله عن يمينه وعن شماله وخلفه فلا يرى إلا الشجر والحجارة فمكث كذلك يرى ويسمع ما شاء ما أن يمكث

from Jabir bin Samurah, that the Messenger of Allah said: "Indeed in Mecca there is a rock that used to give me Salam during the night of my advent, and I can identify it even now." Jami` at-Tirmidhi Vol. 1, Book 46, Hadith 3624

Allah's Messenger as said: *I recognize the stone in Mecca which used to pay me salutations before my advent as a Prophet and I recognize that even now.* Sahih Muslim 2277

The prophet asking his donkey about sex!

"When Allah opened Khaybar to his prophet Muhammad – may Allah's prayers

and salute him, he (Muhammad) received as his share of the spoils four sheep, four goats, ten pots of gold and silver and a black, haggard donkey.

The prophet – may Allah's prayers and salute and him addressed the donkey asking, 'What is your name?' the donkey replied, 'Yazid Ibn Shihab. Allah had brought forth from my ancestry sixty donkeys, none of whom were ridden on except by prophets of Allah including prophet 'Isa. None of the descendants of my grandfather remain but me, and none of the prophets remain but you and I expected you to ride me. Before you, I used to be owned by a Jewish man, whom I caused to stumble and fall often so he used to kick my stomach and beat my back.' The prophet – may Allah's prayers and salute him said: to him, 'I will call you Ya'foor, Oh Ya'foor.' Then Ya'foor replied, 'I obey.' The prophet then asked, 'Do you desire females?' The donkey replied, 'No I don't like females!'

So the prophet used to ride the donkey to do his work and if the prophet dismounted from him he would send the donkey to the house of the person he wanted to visit and Ya'foor would knock at the door with his head. When the owner of the house would answer the door, the donkey would signal to that person to go see the prophet. When the prophet died, the donkey went to a well belonging to Abu Al-Haytham Ibn Al-Tahyan and threw himself in the well out of sadness for the prophet's death, making it his grave." Kathir Al Bidaya Wal Nihaya volume 9, page 49.

لما فتح الله على نبيه صلى الله عليه وسلم خيبر أصابه من سهمه أربعة أزواج نعال وأربعة أزواج خفاف ، وعشر أواق ذهب وفضة ، وحمار أسود ، ومكتل . قال : فكلم النبي صلى الله عليه وسلم الحمار ، فكلمه الحمار ، فقال له : « ما اسمك؟ » قال : « يزيد بن شهاب ، أخرج الله [ص: 42] من نسل جدي ستين حمارا ، كلهم لم يركبهم إلا نبي ، ولم يبق من نسل جدي غيري ، ولا من الأنبياء غيرك ، وقد كنت أتوقعك أن تركبني ، قد كنت قبلك لرجل يهودي ، وكنت أعثر به عمدا ، وكان يجيع بطني ويضرب ظهري ، فقال له النبي صلى الله عليه وسلم : « قد سميتك يعفورا ، يا يعفور » . قال : لبيك . قال « أتشتهي الإناث؟ » قال : لا . فكان النبي صلى الله عليه وسلم يركبه لحاجته ، فإذا نزل عنه بعث به إلى باب الرجل ، فيأتي الباب فيقرعه برأسه ، فإذا خرج إليه صاحب الدار أوما إليه أن أجب رسول الله صلى الله عليه وسلم ، فلما قبض النبي صلى الله عليه وسلم جاء إلى بئر كانت لأبي الهيثم بن التيهان ، فتردى فيها فصارت قبره: جزعا منه على رسول الله صلى الله عليه وسلم

If you're a believer, then you believe in miracles, however I find this story very funny and very naïve, if I am a man, for the first time ever speaking to an animal do you think I'm going to ask him questions:

- ↬ About its sexuality?
- ↬ And hold on the donkey after the prophet asked his donkey: do you like females we got an astonishing answer. **"The prophet then asked, 'Do you desire females?' The donkey replied, 'No I don't like females!'"**
- ↬ It is a donkey but yet it is a gay!

◇ The prophet's donkey committed suicide!

I have no more comments to add, you be the judge!

Muhammad Trying to Commit Suicide

One of the advanced symptoms of epilepsy is suicidal thoughts, and obviously he tried to do so many times as we read together:

" *Waraqa died, and the Inspiration was also paused for a while and the Prophet came to be so sad as we have heard that he intended several times to throw himself from the heads of high mountains and every time he went up the top of a mountain in order to throw himself down." Gabriel would appear in front him and say, "O Muhammad! You are indeed Allah's Messenger in truth" whereupon his heart would become calm and he would calm down and would return home. And at whatever time the period of the coming of the inspiration used to become long, he would do as before, but when he used to reach the top of a mountain, Gabriel would appear before him and say to him what he had said before."* Sahih al-Bukhari 6982

There's few books written by Muslims speaking of the life Muhammad before and after he claimed to be a prophet here's a quote from the book of Al Siarah Al-'Halabia volume 1-page number 360: *reported that the prophet before, he started receiving revelation, what he seemed like to be he faint after shaking, while his eyes was closed, and Khadija (his wife she) said: to him should I do some reading (anti-magic statements) for you to protect you? And his face used to turn yellow and he's snore like a camel!*

صلى الله عليه وسلم كان يصيبه قبل نزول القرآن ما يشبه الإغماء بعد حصول الرعدة، وتغميض عينيه، وتربد وجهه، ويغط كغطيط البكر، فقالت له خديجة: أوجه إليك من يرقيك؟ قال: أما الآن فلا» ولم أقف على من كان يرقيه ولا على ما كان يرقى به.

1. As you see these are exactly the symptoms of epilepsy.
2. But because at that time the people didn't understand what was happening, therefore they used to consider any person with such symptoms and illness, under the influence of magic or envy.

Dr. Muhammad Ghali's translation of Qur'an 113:

1. Say, "I take refuge with The Lord of the Daybreak, (Literally: The Splitting "of the day").
2. From the evil of whatever He has created,

3. And from the evil of darkness when it settles
4. And from the evil of the women who spit on the knots, (i.e., perform malignant witchcraft).
5. And from the evil of an envier when he envies."

It's so clear that he is acknowledging by this chapter that he has a problem but he thinks it is due to black magic and the practice of Secret arts or envy.

Allah's Messenger said, "He who eats seven 'Ajwa dates fruits every morning, will not be affected by poison or magic in the day he eats it." Sahih al-Bukhari 5445

And I find it very dramatic that Muhammad became an expert or a doctor and gave prescriptions about how to fight envy or black magic, yet he himself is suffering from the problem which according to him is black magic, and at the end of his life he was killed by poison!

The Prophet at his illness in which he died, used to say, "O 'Aisha! I still feel the pain caused by the food I ate at Khaibar, and at this time, I feel as if my aorta is being cut from that poison." Sahih al-Bukhari 4428

Many times, more he perceived what's supposed to be an angel and he came back to his wife we read this:

Allah's Messenger came back with the Inspiration, his body was trembling, his neck and muscles were shaking with terror till he entered upon Khadija and said, "Cover me! Cover me!" They covered him till his fear was over and then he said, "O Khadija, what is wrong with me?" Sahih al-Bukhari 6982/ Book 65, Hadith 4953

One of the symptoms of staged epilepsy is that the patient might hear very ans noying noises like sound of the ring of the bell:

Al Harith bin Hisham enquired into the Prophet, "How does the divine inspiration come to you?" He answered "In all these ways: The Angel from time to time comes to me with a voice which resembles the sound like a ringing bell, and when this state separates me, and then I comprehend what the Angel has said, and this type of Divine Inspiration is the hardest on me; and from time to time the Angel comes to me in the shape of a man and talks to me, and I understand what he says." Sahih al-Bukhari 3215 call

a. Have you ever heard of someone who was a prophet and he received inspiration as the sound of the bell which was very harsh on him?
b. How the voice of an angel became a sound of a bell?

c. How Muhammad was able to translate the sound of the bell into Arabic?

d. And what makes it more funny and strange is that Muhammad said: the bell is a sound and the musical instrument of the devil! And angels hate both bell and flute!

"Abu Hurairah reported the Apostle of Allah as saying "The bell and wooden flute are musical instrument of Satan." Sunan Abi Dawud 2556/ Sahih Muslim 2113 a

Abu Hurairah reported the Apostle of Allah as saying "The angels do not accompany the fellow travelers who have a dog or bell (with them)." Sunan Abi Dawud 2555

And the fact is one of the symptoms of epilepsy is contradictory of talk and logic. The fact is, because he was seriously ill at the end of his life they mocked him and disobeyed him as we read:

Ibn `Abbas said: *"When the ailment of Allah prophet became worse, he said, 'Bring for me a paper and I will write for you a declaration after which you will not go astray.' But `Umar said, 'The Prophet is seriously ill, and we have got Allah's Book with us and that is sufficient for us.' But the companions of the Prophet disagreed about this and there was a chaos and yell. On that the Prophet said to them, "leave me alone. It is not right that you should fight in front of me." Ibn `Abbas came out saying, "It was most disastrous that Allah's Messenger was prevented from writing that statement for them because of their disagreement and noise.* Sahih al-Bukhari 114

After this introduction to the health issue which obviously Muhammad is suffering from, we go back to learn more details about sexuality and Islam, which is so important to understand the background of the one who established this religion and its rules.

The dirty language of the prophet and his leaders

"somebody is a proud about his pre-Heritage before Islam insult him, and tell him to go on and bite the penis of his father" Al-Jam' Al-Sageer V.1, p 47

الجامع الصغير من حديث البشير النذير - باب: حرف الألف ج١ ص47
إذا رأيتم الرجل يتعزى بعزاء الجاهلية فأعضوه بهن أبيه ولا تكنوا -
يتعزى ": ينتسب "]
" فأعضوه أي فاشتموه قائلين: « عض بذكر أبيك
" والهن هو الذكر، أي الفرج كما في « القاموس » وكما في « النهاية

The Prophet said: *"If somebody is approachable as a pre-Heritage before Islam bite his penis and don't call him with respect"* Al-Adab Al-Mufrad 963

سَمِعْتُ النَّبِيَّ صلى الله عليه وسلم يَقُولُ: مَنْ تَعَزَّى بِعَزَاءِ الْجَاهِلِيَّةِ فَأَعِضُوهُ وَلَا تَكْنُوهُ

What did Muhammad hear and see at his daughter's wedding?

The coming story if it is truly told by Muhammad, then we can add it to list of the madness symptoms he was suffering from: *When the night of wedding (of Fatima) the prophet he brought his white mule and cover it with a piece of fabric, and he told Fatima to ride on it, ordering Solomon to lead the mule, and while he is in the way he heard a sound, and it was Gabriel (the angel) with 70,000 angel, and the Angel Mikael with other 70,000 angels the prophet said: " what do brought you here to earth?" They said (the Angels) we came to attend the wedding of Fatima to her husband, and therefore the angel Gabriel said "Allah Akbar", and the Angel Mikael said: "Allah Akbar", therefore since then it became a tradition in the wedding night to shout Allah Akbar.* Wasel Al-Shia [25116] 4.

فلما كان ليلة الزفاف اتى النبي (صلى الله عليه وآله) ببغلته الشهباء وثنى عليها قطيفة ، وقال لفاطمة : اركبي ، وأمر سلمان أن يقودها ، والنبي (صلى الله عليه وآله) يسوقها ، فبينما هو في بعض الطريق إذ سمع النبي (صلى الله عليه وآله) وجبة (١) ، فإذا بجبريل في سبعين ألفا وميكائيل في سبعين ألفا ، فقال النبي (صلى الله عليه وآله) : ما أهبطكم إلى الارض ؟ فقالوا : جئنا نزف فاطمة إلى زوجها ، وكبر جبرئيل وكبر ميكائيل وكبرت الملائكة وكبر محمد (صلى الله عليه وآله) ، فوضع التكبير على العرائس من تلك الليلة .

I have to admit that I wish the smartphone existed during that time, and I would have been there, not because I would like to record the event of 140,000 angels attending a wedding, but to take a selfie with such a crowded number of angels! However I was wondering how a small town like Mecca was able to fit such a huge number, and as you know each one of them has 600 wings and covers the horizon!

"I asked Zir bin Hubaesh about the saying of Allah : And was a distance of two bow lengths or less (Qur'an 53:9). So he said: 'Ibn Mas'ud told me that the Prophet saw Gabriel, and he had six-hundred wings.' Jami` at-Tirmidhi Vol. 5, Book 44, Hadith 3277.

(He saw him) One time at Sidrat Al-Muntaha and one time in with horses and he(the angel) had six-hundred wings which filled the horizon."' Jami` at-Tirmidhi Vol. 5, Book 44, Hadith 3278.

And that reminds me of Muhammad's statement about a flying creature between the size of a donkey and the size of a mule, and when he told his people about his flying, they accused him of fabrication, and then he suddenly stood up to start describing Jerusalem for them!

Narrated Jabir bin `Abdullah: *That he heard Allah's Messenger saying, "When the people of Quraish did not believe me (i.e. the story of my Night flying Journey), I stood up in Al-Hijr (Rocky location) and Allah displayed Jerusalem in front of me, and I began describing it to them while I was looking at it."* Sahih al-Bukhari 3886

Now I am not sure if you can see with me how funny this story is, so let's look closely at the following:

- Muhammad already claimed that he had been in Jerusalem.
- His people could not believe him because he did not leave town.
- But yet he said: "and Allah displayed Jerusalem in front of me, and I began describing it to them while I was looking at it."
- But why does he need Allah to display it in the front of him so he can dee scribe, when in fact he should describe what he saw from his memory?
- Imagine I said to you I went to Hong Kong, and then you say to me: okay describe it I don't believe you! Then Allah displays Hong Kong in front of my eyes, so I would be able to describe it to you, but if I was there already I do not need the help of Allah, in order to be able to describe it to you, do I?
- If the story is true, I mean what Muhammad is reporting that he saw a display of Jerusalem while he is between his people, then there's only one possible explanation, and that is, he must be delusional and suffering from a mental illness.

However we get more clear proof about the false trip to heaven from his wife who at that specific night was in the bed with Muhammad where she said: *One of Abu Bakr's family told me that 'Aisha, the Prophet's wife, used to say: "The apostle's body remained where it was but God removed his spirit by night".* Ibn Ishaq, Sirat Rasulullah, p. 183. Ibn Hisham 2/46. Al Tabrai 22175, 14/445

Which means this complete story of Muhammad was not true and was not even believed by his wife, but to cover his lies or his illusion she said "The apostle's body remained where it was but God removed his spirit by night"

***

Jihad for the sake of Blondies!

We always hear a lot of arguments about jihad, and the word in Arabic means hard struggle, however today we will speak about the sexual jihad.

And one of the verses of the Quran: *"And among them is he who says: "Grant me leave (to be exempted from Jihad) and do not tempt us (by women).".*" Surely, they have fallen into trial. And verily, Hell is surrounding the disbelievers."* – Quran 9:49

By the authority of interpretation of Imam Al –'Tbari: *That the prophet Said: regarding the Quran 9:49 "Grant me leave (to be exempted from Jihad) and put me not into trial." He said (the prophet): "attack the city of Tabuk have you would Capture the Blondie girls"* so a man his name Al-jad said: *"Grant me leave (to be exempted from Jihad) and put me not into trial. "Grant me leave (to be exempted from Jihad) and do not tempt us by women."* Al'Tabari volume 14 Page 287

حدثني محمد بن عمرو ، قال: ثنا أبو عاصم، قال: ثنا عيسى، عن ابن أبي نجيح، عن مجاهد، في
قول الله: { انْذَنْ لِي وَلا تَفْتِنِّي } قال: قال رسول الله صلى الله عليه وسلم: « اغْزُوا تُبُوكَ تَغْنَمُوا بَناتِ
الأصْفَر وَنِساءَ الرُّوم » فقال الجدّ: انذن لنا، ولا تفتنا بالنساء.
حدثنا القاسم، قال: ثنا الحسين، قال: ثني حجاج، عن ابن جريج، عن مجاهد، قالوا: قال رسول الله
صلى الله عليه وسلم: « اغْزُوا تَغْنَمُوا بَناتِ الأصْفَر » يعني: نساء الروم، ثم ذكر مثله.

I saw many articles written by Muslims, trying to defend such a statement, and the excuse was that the prophet is attacking Syria because the Romans occupied Syria, but in fact the Romans were there more than 1000 years before Muhammad. Even the Quran speaks of Allah who would give them victory over the Persian, during the lifetime of Muhammad and the Muslims named the chapter after the Romans!

1. L. M. (don't be surprised, Muslims don't know what this means)
2. The Roman Empire had already been defeated
3. In a land close by; but they, (even though) after this defeat of theirs, they will soon be victorious! Within a few years. With Allah is the Decision, in the past and in the Future: on that Day shall the Believers rejoice Quran 30

As you see it was Allah who made them victorious in Syria, and even Allah claimed that the Romans are believers which means they are Muslims, and soon those Muslim Roman believers, would rejoice for the victories against the pagan Persians.

This is why these kind of articles, written by Muslims show their ignorance about what is written in their books.

And the question is if, like the Muslims always claim, the prophet was giving an order to do jihad to defend himself. But if you read the chapter you will find that he is just attacking to earn money and women, and from his own mouth he explained to his men, what the benefit is of doing jihad namely capturing the Blondie women and rape them. Subsequently, when a decent man said to him don't tempt us by blondie women, we see Mohammed calling him a hypocrite!

Go suck the clitoris of Al-Lat?

And here's one of the stories about the argument between the Muslims and the people of Mecca. The companion of Muhammad Abu Baker the father of 'Aisha said: "Go and suck the clitoris of Allat". Sahih al-Bukhari 2731, 2732

فَقَالَ لَهُ أَبُو بَكْرٍ امْصُصْ بَظْرَ اللَّاتِ،

If we read the Muslims' translation, you would notice immediately how they hide all those bad words in the English version and that is why you should not trust any Islamic text translated by Muslims.

When Ma'iz bin Malik came to the Prophet, the Prophet said to him, "Probably you have only kissed her, or winked, or looked at her?" He said, "No, O Allah's Messenger. The Prophet they have the proper therefore the Prophet said, "Did you Fuck her?" أَنِكْتَهَا *then the Prophet ordered that he be stoned (to death). Sahih al-Bukhari 6824.*

حَدَّثَنِي عَبْدُ اللَّهِ بْنُ مُحَمَّدٍ الْجُعْفِيُّ، حَدَّثَنَا وَهْبُ بْنُ جَرِيرٍ، حَدَّثَنَا أَبِي قَالَ، سَمِعْتُ يَعْلَى بْنَ حَكِيمٍ، عَنْ عِكْرِمَةَ، عَنِ ابْنِ عَبَّاسٍ ـ رضى الله عنهما ـ قَالَ لَمَّا أَتَى مَاعِزُ بْنُ مَالِكٍ النَّبِيَّ صلى الله عليه وسلم قَالَ لَهُ « لَعَلَّكَ قَبَّلْتَ أَوْ غَمَزْتَ أَوْ نَظَرْتَ ». قَالَ لاَ يَا رَسُولَ اللَّهِ. قَالَ « أَنِكْتَهَا ». قَالَ لاَ يَكْنِي. قَالَ فَعِنْدَ ذَلِكَ أَمَرَ بِرَجْمِهِ.

I am really sorry if I used very harsh language in my translation, but because I have to be honest and the whole purpose of this book is to share the truth exactly as it is without any political correctness.

SEXUALITY IN THE EYES OF ALLAH

For sure when we say sexuality in the eyes of Allah, I mean in the eyes of Muhammad. The duty of women in this life and the hereafter: The duty of women in this life.

The Quran is full of verses speaking of the duty of the Muslim women, and it's so clear that it consists of a combination of two:

-ↄ Sex and Joy for the man
-ↄ Delivering children to spread Islam.

Your wives are as a tilth unto you; so, approach your tilth when or how ye will; but do some good act for your souls beforehand; and fear Allah. And know that ye are to meet Him (in the Hereafter) and give (these) good tidings to those who believe. Q 2:223 Youssef Ali trans.

The thing which we would notice in Islam is that the author of the Quran always speaks to men what they can do with women, however the prophet of Islam gives orders for both, and when it comes to sex women are always the ones to blame, for it is a duty to satisfy the sexual needs of the men, and it's not the other way around.

"The Prophet said, "If a woman spends the night abandoning her husband's bed (does not have sex with him), then the angels send their curses on her till she comes back to bed" Sahih al-Bukhari 5194.

So are the women to blame if they are avoiding having sex with the husband for some reason, like maybe being upset, sad, don't feel like it, etc. According to Islam, the angels of Allah would curse this woman for she is not doing her duty, which she is created for, as a sex pleasure provider for the man.

However, the man he has no obligation and angels will not curse him if he abandons the bed of any of his wives, he was in fact encouraged to punish women by abandoning their beds additional to beating and be harsh solution.

Men are in charge of women, because Allah hath made the one of them to excel the other, and because they spend of their property (for the support of women). So, good women are the obedient, guarding in secret that which Allah hath guarded. As for those from whom ye fear rebellion, admonish them and banish them to beds apart, and scourge them. Then if they obey you, seek not a way against them. Lo! Allah is ever High, Exalted, Great. Q 4:34 Pickthall's Translation.

Which means a Muslim man can use sexuality as a punishment to any of his wives just as he pleases, to "correct her behavior". And don't forget men have many options, I mean sexual options, Muslim men may have many wives, and sex slaves, while women can have only one husband.

CHRISTIAN PRINCE – SEX AND ALLAH VOLUME 1

And it doesn't not matter if the wife is good or bad, the man can sleep with her whenever he wishes. Or even ignore her forever if he wishes, as Muhammad did with his wife Sauda, who never did anything wrong yet he does not like to sleep with her and wants to get rid of her.

Young versus old women and sex

Millions of times I heard Muslims speaking about the justice of the prophet of Islam, and today we are going to examine his sexual justice. When one of his wives became old, Muhammad abandoned this woman, for no reason except that she is not the prettiest compared to the other wives he had.

When the the second wife of Muhammad, Sauda, became old, and Muhammad stopped coming to her house, she was afraid that he was going to divorce her soon, and he is not coming to see her no more, so to avoid being homeless, she has nothing and nowhere to go, and because she knew that he favors the youngest wife 'Aisha the one he married at the age of six, she offered 'Aisha a deal, convince him not to divorce me and I will give you my day which is supposedly her right as a wife to spend with Muhammad:

'Aisha said: Never did I find any woman more loving to me than Sauda bint Zam'a. I wished I could be exactly like her who was passionate. As she became old, she had made over her day (which used to be scheduled to spend with Muhammad) to 'A'isha. She said: I gave my day to you to 'A'isha. So, Allah's Messenger assigned two days to 'A'isha, her own day and that of Sauda. Sahih Muslim 1463 a

If you read this quotation above, you might think that this was a choice of the old women the fact it's not we find in the Quran:

If a wife fears cruelty or desertion on her husband's part, there is no blame on them if they arrange an amicable settlement between themselves; and such settlement is best; even though men's souls are swayed by greed. But if ye do good and practice self-restraint, Allah is well-acquainted with all that ye do. Q 2:128 Yusuf Ali Trans.

As you see this man always used his god to legalize every simple action he does in order to avoid any criticism because of unjust behavior. Look at the way he deals with this old woman, imagine this woman she spent many years with him, but now because he got many women, which are younger, prettier, he decides to dump her, and he found the solution which is: let's give an extra day to my favorite wife 'Aisha.

"*Sauda feared that the Prophet was going to divorce her, so she said: 'Do not divorce me, but keep me and give my day to 'Aisha.' So, he did so, and the following was revealed from Allah: Then there is no sin on them both if they make terms of peace between themselves, and making peace is better (4:128). So, whatever they agree to make peace in something then it is permissible.*" Jami' at-Tirmidhi Vol. 5, Book 44, Hadith 3040.

1. As you see from the above story, this was not an agreement as much as it was the last choice for this old woman.
2. After she announced her fear that he might divorce her, Muhammad did not deny that he is going to do so, which means he was one step far from divorcing this woman.
3. And if we read the quotation "(4:128). So, whatever they agree to make peace in something then it is permissible."
4. That would lead us, that there was a fight over this issue, and finally when the old woman (Sauda) noticed that she is losing ground, and he would divorce her, she gives up her right as a wife, for the sake of security and not to be homeless.
5. The simple conclusion of this, women can be dumped after being used and abused, and the Muslim man's god is always at his side.

As long as we mentioned it already, beating as a punishment is something the man can always choose to do to his wives.

Can the man beat his wife if she refuses to share the bed? In the coming story we will see the answer for this question.

Beating wife if she refuses sex

Rifa'a divorced his wife whereupon 'Abd Al-Rahman bin Al-Zubair Al-Qurazi married her. 'Aisha said that the lady which is wearing a green veil and complained to her (Aisha) of her husband and showed her a green spot on her skin caused by beating. It was the normal practice of women's backing each other, so when Allah's Messenger came, 'Aisha said, "I have not seen any woman suffering as much as the believing women. Look! Her skin is greener than her clothes!" When 'Abd Al-Rahman heard that his wife had gone to the Prophet, he came with his two sons from another wife. She said, "By Allah! I have done no wrong to him but he is sexually powerless and is as useless to me as this," holding and showing the fringe of her garment, 'Abd Al-Rahman said, "By Allah, O Allah's Messenger! She has told a lie! I am very strong and can satisfy her but she is disobedient and wants to go back to Rifa`a." Allah's Messenger said, to her, "If that is your objective, then know that it is unlawful for you to remarry Rifa`a unless 'Abd Al-Rahman he taste you're a juice (has had sexual intercourse with you)." Then the Prophet saw two boys with ` Abd Al-Rahman and asked (him), "Are these your sons?" On that 'Abd Al-Rahman said, "Yes." The Prophet said, "You claim what you claim (i.e.. that he is sexually useless)? But by Allah, these boys resemble him as a crow resembles a crow". Sahih al-Bukhari 5825.

To make the story simple, regardless who is telling the truth in the story the wife or the husband:

- ⊷ The man did beat his wife.
- ⊷ To the point that the skin became greener than her clothes.
- ⊷ And the fight is over sex.
- ⊷ And all along Muhammad took the side of the man.
- ⊷ That means the fight was about the wife rejecting to sleep with the husband, so the husband did beat her, and the prophet had no problem with that at all.
- ⊷ On top of that Muhammad gives her a warning that if it's her objective to go back to her previous husband, she cannot do so unless the current husband tastes her juice.

The new husband must taste your juice.

One of the mad sexual practices Muhammad established, was that if a man dit vorced his wife three times, and this man or his divorced wife would like to get back together, they cannot do so unless the divorced wife sleeps with a new man, and this new man has to taste her juice, and she has to taste his juice.

Notice with me please, I'm not trying to use dirty language, I am just translating exactly what Muhammad said.

"The wife of Rifa'ah Al-Qurzi came to the Messenger of Allah and said: 'I was with Rifa'ah and he divorced me permanently (three times). Then I married Abdur-Rahman bin Az-Zubair, but he only has the likes of the fringe of a garment.' So he said: 'Perhaps you want me to return to Rifa'ah? No, not until you taste his juice, and he tastes your juice.'" Jami` at-Tirmidhi 1118.

And as usual Muhammad right away created what Muslims call revelations reh garding this issue.

So, if he divorces her she shall not be lawful to him afterwards until she had sexual intercourse with another husband; then if he divorces her there is no blame on them both if they return to each other (wife go back to the previous husband), if they think that they can keep within the limits of Allah, and these are the limits of Allah which He makes clear for a people who know. Q 2:230

- ✦ Imagine how crazy to say to someone that if you divorced your wife three times, you cannot have her back unless she is going to have sex with another husband.
- ✦ In the Muslims translation, we find 'remarries her', instead it is sexual intercourse with her, that verse is already stating that you have to marry a new husband, under the condition that "he tastes her juice, and she tastes his juice", which is simply a statement of sexual intercourse but in dirty street language.

To be fair I will show you the Muslims answering a question about this issue and I quote: https://islamqa.info/en/167255

"I do not know why Islam does not allow the man to marry his wife again if he has divorced her then he wants to take her back. The Qur'an states that she has to marry another man first, then only after that can the first husband marry her again. That does not seem logical to me; rather I think it is harsh."

The scholars' answer: "If the man, every time he divorced his wife, was able to make a new marriage contract with her and take her back, a man might divorce his wife dozens of times, and each time he would be harming her and breaking her heart, then people of goodwill would try to reconcile between them, or the woman might feel sorry for her children, so she goes back to her husband. This is obviously unfair and unjust to her.

But if the husband knows that the third divorce will make his wife irrevocably divorced from him, in the sense that he will not be able to take her back until after she has married another man who then dies or divorces her, but he may not die or divorce her, then he would be afraid of divorce and would keep away from it, and he would not resort to it except in cases of necessity or urgent need. In that there is mercy for the wife and protection for the family, and it prevents people being heedless about the matter or toying with it."

End of quotation

So, based on the answers of the scholars of Islam, it was a way to stop the man from abusing his right to divorce, and Allah comes with such super intelligent way to stop the man from doing so. If that was for the benefit of the women, why the man has the right to divorce up to three times, what about making the divorce once and for all, as long as you told him he can do it up to three times as if I am saying this is a game with 3 trials so after that: game over. And the Muslims until now still divorce their wives three times and the rule did not stop them from abusing the right of divorce, additional to that the third one is the final for her, not for him, which means she is the one who should get married to a new husband, she is the one who will be suffering again, because now in order to get back to her children and to the previous husband, she has got to sleep with a strange man and he has to "taste her juice", and she has to "taste his juice".

So, what is the wisdom in that?

It is the women again paying the price from her life and with pain, because this god Allah gave the man the right to abuse.

If the divorce is something harmful for women as the Muslim scholar just said in his answer, why are Allah & Muhammad making it so easy for the man to divorce?

In fact, nowadays Muslims can divorce their wives by text messages.

I quote from the BBC News *"The government's adviser on religious affairs, the man who counsels Malaysia's Prime Minister Mahathir Mohamad, said as long as the message was clear and unambiguous it was valid under Islamic Sharia law."*

- And here I would like to ask, why it's so easy for the man to get rid of the woman but is it the same for the woman to get rid of the man?
- Why the can the man force his wife into bed, but the woman cannot force her husband into bed?
- Why you have the right to have four wives, but she cannot have four husbands.
- The man could sleep with as many slaves he owned, but the Muslim woman cannot sleep with the slaves as many as she owns.

In the previous Hadith, we noticed that woman whose husband beat her until her skin became green. What was her reason to marry a new husband? It was to get back to the old husband.

And as a result, she was beaten by the new husband, and Muhammad is forcing her to sleep with the new man, if she likes to go back to the former husband!

Which is nothing but an approval of rape, because the story makes very clear that she is refusing to sleep with the man which is the new husband, she is using a false excuse to avoid the sexual intercourse, then she was beaten and the prophet of Islam took the side of the husband approving the man's aggression and violence. Muslims always tried to deceive us by saying that you can beat your wife lightly, but the story was so clear: wasn't the woman's skin greener than her clothes? Yet she was the wrong one, and the husband was acting according to Allah's teaching.

There are hundreds of movies made in Islamic countries, making fun of that stupid Law of Allah, about true life stories of millions of Muslims, after divorcing their wives for the third time, they go and look for a "husband" to marry their divorced wives, for a one night stand and be sure he would have sexual intercourse with her, and they pay him for such a service, so they can get their divorcee back legally according Islamic Sharia Law!

Hypocrisy of Muhammad

So, divorce was made as easy for the man, as it was to marry additional wives, in the coming story we'll see the hypocrisy of Muhammad, when it's come to his daughter's husband trying to marry a second wife, look what he did:

"While he was on the stage, I heard the Prophet saying: 'Indeed Banu Hisham bin Al-Mughirah asked for my permission if they could marry their daughter to 'Ali bin Abi Talib(the husband of his own daughter). But I do not allow it, I do not allow it, I do not allow it - unless 'Ali bin Abi Talib wishes to divorce my daughter and marry their daughter, because she is a part of me. I am displeased by what displeases her, and I am harmed by what harms her." Jami` at-Tirmidhi Vol. 1, Book 46, Hadith 3867.

- So just because she is his daughter, he will not allow his son in law to practice his Islamic right to multiply his wives as he wishes.
- And he demands that he will not allow such a marriage to happen, unless 'Ali first divorces his daughter.
- And what is the reason he demanded first the divorce, look what he said: "because she is a part of me. I am displeased by what displeases her, and I am harmed by what harms her."
- Which means, he admitted that allowing the man to marry additional wives is nothing but harm for the first wife, yes, he has no problem with it whatsoever, he had endless numbers of women, but when it is about his daughter's hus-

band wanting to have more wives, Muhammad was so upset he objected three times, to confirm to the crowd how much he was against it.

No sex during women's menstruation

They ask thee concerning women's courses. Say: They are a hurt and a pollution: So, keep away from women in their courses, and do not approach them until they are clean. But when they have purified themselves, ye may approach them in any manner, time, or place ordained for you by Allah. For Allah loves those who turn to Him constantly and He loves those who keep themselves pure and clean. Q2:222 Yusuf Ali Translation.

When you read this verse for the first time it sounds good, decent. Islam has two faces, something we usually describe as hypocrisy. While this prophet used to order his men to stay away from their wives during menstruation, was schooling his people about good manners, right and wrong, he himself was doing the opposite:

Maimunah the daughter of Al Harith said "When the Apostle of Allah intended to have sex and lie with any of his wives who was menstruating, he ordered her to wrap up what piece of cloth then he had sexual relationship with her. Sunan Abi Dawud 2167.

Aisha said: "Whenever Allah's Messenger wanted to have sex with anyone of us during her top time of her menses, he used to order her to put on small sheet and start sexual relationship with her." 'Aisha added, "None of you could control his sexual desires as the Prophet could!!!" Sahih al-Bukhari 302.

I find that this is very disgusting, and a clear sign of hypocrisy. Why a man owning many sex slaves, dozens of wives waiting for him in the bedrooms, would go and harass a woman during her menstruation?

But the disgusting story turned to be very funny when Muhammad's wife 'Aisha said "None of you could control his sexual desires as the Prophet could!!!"

What kind of control he had? With other wives and concubines waiting in the bedroom all waiting for his majesty, couldn't he control himself and have sex with one of those women?

Science & sex in Islam

Why Allah made Women's menstrual period?

It was reported from Abu Ja'far Muhammad bin Ali peace up on him he said: " the women in the time of Noah used to have menstrual period once a year, and Until about 700 women Took off their veil, and start wearing clothing with Colors and wearing jewelry and perfume, and afterward they went out and spread around the land and this set and associate themselves with men, therefore Allah cursed them with menstrual period every month, and that was a curse for exact women(the 700 who did that), and their blood start running, and afterward they separated themselves from the man, and Allah kept them busy with their menstrual period, and He broke their desire.

In the same time the other women(the good women) were having one menstrual period a year still, but because the children over those women they married from the children of the women who have monthly menstrual period, the numbers of the children of the monthly menstrual period overcome the others therefore all women today had monthly menstrual period. Tafsir Nur Al-'Thakalen here too 808.

في كتاب علل الشرايع باسناده إلى أبي عبيدة الحذاء عن أبي جعفر محمد بن علي عليه السلام قال: -
.الحيض من النساء نجاسة رماهن الله بها قال
وقد كن النساء في زمن نوح انما تحيض المراة في كل سنة حيضة حتى خرجن نسوة من حجابهن
.وهن سبعمائة امرأة فانطلقن فلبسن المعصفرات من الثياب وتحلين وتعطرن
.ثم خرجن فتفرقن في البلاد فجلسن مع الرجال وشهدن الأعياد معهم وجلسن في صفوفهم
.فرماهن الله بالحيض عند ذلك في كل شهر، أولئك النسوة بأعيانهن
فسالت دماءهن فخرجن من بين الرجال وكن يحضن في كل شهر حيضة قال، فاشغلهن الله تبارك
وتعالى بالحيض وكسر شهوتهن، قال: وكان غيرهن من النساء اللواتي لم يفعلن مثل فعلهن يحضن في
كل سنة حيضة قال: فتزوج بنوا اللاتي يحضن في كل شهر حيضة بنات اللاتي يحضن في كل سنة
حيضة، قال: فامتزج القوم فحضن بنات هؤلاء وهؤلاء في كل شهر حيضة، قال: وكثر أولاد اللاتي
يحضن في كل شهر حيضة لاستقامة الحيض، وقل أولاد الذين لا يحضن في السنة الا حيضة لفساد
.الدم، قال: وكثر نسل هؤلاء وقل نسل أولئك

The Caliph examining the private part of the Child daughter of Ali

We mentioned already that Muhammad had a sexual desire for children this is why he got married to 'Aisha but it's clear that all followers of Muhammad follow in his footsteps.

From Abi Ja'far he said: 'Umar ibn Al-Kha'tab asked for permission to marry the daughter of Ali, but Ali said she is so young, therefore some said to 'Umar he is using that as an excuse so you will not have her, so 'Umar told him about that(what they said), therefore Ali said: alright I was sent out to you and your check her out if you accept her she's your wife, afterward he send her to him(to 'Umar) and then 'Umar exposed her leg(by lifting up her skirt) therefore she said(the child daughter of Ali) let it go(the skirt) if you are not the caliph I will chop your head! Book of Mu'sanaf Abd Al-Razaq book of Nikah (Book of sexual intercourse) hadith 10352.

عبد الرزاق ، عن ابن عيينة ، عن عمرو بن دينار ، عن أبي جعفر قال : خطب عمر إلى 10352 علي ابنته ، فقال : إنها صغيرة ، فقيل لعمر : إنما يريد بذلك منعها قال : فكلمه ، فقال علي : « أبعث بها إليك ، فإن رضيت فهي امرأتك » قال : فبعث بها إليه قال : فذهب عمر فكشف ، عن ساقها ، فقالت : أرسل ، فلولا أنك أمير المؤمنين لصككت عنقك

Fatima Muhammad's daughter is menstrual period free!

It was reported by Abi Ja'far peace upon him said: Allah sealed her with knowledge and made her menstruation free! And Imam Al-Majlsee the first confirmed that this is a Strong story (authentic). Book of Al-Asrar Al-Fa'temeah page 391. Bihar Al-Anwar, volume 10. Al Kafi, Volume 1/381.

وفي رواية عن أبي جعفر : « فسماها فاطمة ، ثم قال : إني فطمتك بالعلم ، وفطمتك عن الطمث » ، ثم قال أبو جعفر عليه السلام : والله ، لقد فطمها الله تبارك وتعالى بالعلم ، وعن الطمث بالميثاق (2) وقد وصف المجلسي الأول هذا الخبر بالقوي

(3)

Book of Al-Asrar Al-Fa'temeah page 391. Bihar Al-Anwar, volume 10. Al Kafi Volume, 1/381.

فاطمة منزهة عن الحيض
عن أبي الحسن قال « إن بنات الأنبياء لا يطمثن » (الكافي 381/1 كتاب الحجة. باب مولد الزهراء فاطمة عليها السلام).
عن أبي جعفر قال » لما ولدت فاطمة عليها السلام أوحى الله إلى ملك فأنطق به لسان محمد رسول الله صلى الله عليه وسلم فسماها فاطمة ثم قال: إني فطمتك بالعلم وفطمتك من الطمث. قال أبو جعفر: والله لقد فطمها عن الطمث في الميثاق« (الكافي 382/1 كتاب الحجة. باب مولد الزهراء عليها السلام).

The gender explanation

I spoke about this hadith before to explore other madness of Muhammad but now we will cover something else.

(A Jewish man said) I have come to ask you about the child. He (the Prophet) said: The water of man is white, and The water of woman yellow, and when they have sexual intercourse and the male's water cum first upon the female's water, it is the *male child that is created by Allah's Decree, and when the water of the female cum first upon the water of the male, a female child is formed by the Decree of Allah. The Jew said: What you have said is true; verily you are an Apostle. He then returned and went away. The Messenger of Allah said: He asked me about such and such things of which I have had no knowledge till Allah gave me that. Sahih Muslim 315 a.*

'Um Salama: 'Um Sulaim said, "O Allah's Apostle! Verily Allah is not shy of the truth. Is it necessary for a woman to take a bath after she had a sexual dream (i.e. discharge from her vagina)" He said, "Yes, if she notices discharge? On that 'Um Salama laughed and said, "Does a woman get a (nocturnal sexual) discharge?" He said, "How then does (her) son resemble her (his mother)?" Sahih Bukhari 3328 Sahih Muslim 313 a.

Sperm is coming from where, women's sperm?

Qur'an 86:6-7
[6] He was created of a gushing fluid
[7] That is issued from between the backs and the ribs.

***

The following interpretation is not ours, this is one of many literal quotations of interpretations by Muslim scholars we provide you with in this book:

The word of creation, it is an answer for a question about where the water is coming from which means the sperm. And it meant to say the two water, the water of the man and the water of the women, because the human is it created from both water. This water come from between the backbone (for the man), Ibn 'Abas said: Al-Tara'ib is the location of the necklace (where the upper side of the ribs meet), which is located between her breasts, and it was narrated by 'Ikrama he said: Al-Tara'ib is the hands and legs. Tafsir Al-Qurtbi volume 20.

. خلق وهو جواب الاستفهام من ماء دافق أي من المني
وأراد مائين : ماء الرجل وماء المرأة ؛ لأن الإنسان مخلوق منهما
يخرج أي هذا الماء من بين الصلب أي الظهر
قال ابن عباس : « الترائب » : موضع القلادة . وعنه : ما بين ثدييها وقال عكرمة . وروي عنه :
يعني ترائب المرأة : اليدين والرجلين

Take a note if you compare between the translation of the same page from Arabic to English at Muslim websites you will see 99% of what is in Al-Qurtbi vanished. Take a look: altafsir.com. For sure the translator is not happy to show such ignorance coming from his god the "almighty".

That issued from between the loins of a man and the ribs of a woman. Tafsir Ibn 'Abas Tanwîr al-Miqbâs

However, what great deal of the following we learned from Allah:

- There is a gushing fluid which happened during the orgasm.
- The gushing fluid contained the sperm of the male and female.
- Women have sperm!
- Women's sperm comes from the upper side of her ribs, which is the location of the necklace!
- The sperm of the man comes from the backbone!
- That was the opinion of the majority of the scholars too.
- 'Ikrama does not agree though, he claims the word Al-Tara'ib stands for the hands and the legs of the woman and this is what Allah meant by that!
- For sure there's nobody in the world no matter how ignorant he might be, who would believe such an explanation made by the god of Islam about the creation of the baby.
- The very famous and well known "Muslim scientist" Abu Baker Al Razi, author of Al Tafsir Al-Kaber page 118 tried his best in his book to defend the Qur'an, so he claimed that the backbone of the man is his brain and he said this is why the newborn baby looks like the brain cells! However not long after that this person became an atheist.

،بل معظم أجزائه إنما يتربى في الدماغ، والدليل عليه أن صورته يشبه الدماغ

How sperm turns into baby?

For sure some of you heard Muslims speaking of science in the Qur'an, and maybe some of you already got my book "Qur'an and Science in Depth". Which is a treasure of reference and information, yet as long as we are speaking about sexual reproduction and biology I have no choice but to mention to you how the Qur'an explained the human reproduction.

Nutfah = Sperm

"Then We made the Nutfah into a clot (a piece of thick coagulated blood), then We made the clot into a little lump of flesh, then We made out of that little lump of flesh bones, then We clothed the bones with flesh, and then We brought it forth as another creation. So Blessed is Allah, the Best of creators. Qur'an 23:14 Muhsen Khan's Translation.

Then, in order to understand this verse in the Qur'an we need to ask the one who made it for the interpretation, which is Muhammad as always:

The Messenger of Allah, and he is the truthful, the honest, recounted to us, "Verily the creation of each one of you is brought together in his mother's womb for forty days in the form of a semen drop, then he becomes a piece of thick coagulated blood ('alaqah) for the equal period(forty days), then a chunk of flesh (mu'dghah) for the same period, then there is sent to him the angel who blows his soul into him and who is commanded with four matters: to write down his fortunate , his life span, his actions, and whether he will be happy or unhappy (i.e., whether he will enter hell of heaven). By the One, other than Whom there is no deity(Allah), verily one of you performs the actions of the people of Paradise until there is but an arm's distance between him and it, and that which has been written overtakes him, and so he acts with the actions of the people of the Hellfire and consequently enters it; and verily one of you acts the actions of the people of the Hellfire, until there is but an arm's length between him and it, and that which has been written(by Allah) overtakes him and so he acts with the actions of the people of Heaven and thus he enters it."
Hadith Nawawi 40 Hadith Nawawi 4

- So according to the prophet of Islam we are created from a drop of sperm that **stays in the womb of the mother for 40 days.**
- But one drop contains millions of semen's, and semen dies in 7 days maximum. The science of prophet Muhammad starts to look like the story of Ali Baba and the 40 thieves.
- Then after that the sperm would become a piece of thick coagulated blood for 40 days, which is absolutely horribly wrong.
- And finally, the piece of thick blood would become a chunk for 40 days. There is no embryonic stage of the baby.
- Which makes a total of 120 days human-being creation!
- But for sure all of this is scientifically rejected, which again proofs Muhammad to be fabricating on his own, claiming that he has been told about all of this by his god.
- From a scientific website we quote "**Since sperm can only live for a maximum of 5 days** in the female reproductive tract, only a small number of sperm will even survive the long journey through the female reproductive tract. Therefore, couples trying to conceive should plan to have intercourse a number of times in the days just prior to ovulation." americanpregnancy.org

To see more stages of embryo development please visit this site which is going to expose the ignorance of the Qur'an's author, which in this case are Muhammad and "Allah". www.babycenter.com/pregnancy-week-by-week

Black people are created for hellfire Muhammad said

Please take a note that the following Hadith is considered Kudsi which means it is holy and equal to the Qur'an, so the Muhammadans cannot say this is weak or rejected, same excuses they always use to run away from any Islamic manuscript exposing the founder of Islam.

Book of Musnad Ahamad, the 10 who've been promised to go to heaven hadith number 26837 (Holy Hadith). *The prophet said: "Allah created Adam on the time of his creation, and he hit him on his right shoulder therefore the race of the white people came to existence as pearls, and He(Allah) hit the left shoulder (of Adam) therefore the black race came to existence as if they are volcano Charcoal, and then He said to the one on the right those are in the right side(the white race) you enter paradise and I don't care, and he said to the those in his left(the black race) hand you go to hell fire and I don't care"*

الكتب » مسند أحمد بن حنبل   » مُسْنَدُ الْعَشَرَةِ الْمُبَشَّرِينَ بِالْجَنَّةِ

رقم الحديث: 26837

(حديث قدسي) حَدَّثَنَا هَيْثَمٌ وَسَمِعْتُهُ أَنَا مِنْهُ , قَالَ : حَدَّثَنَا أَبُو الرَّبِيعِ , عَنْ يُونُسَ , عَنْ أَبِي إِدْرِيسَ , عَنْ) أَبِي الدَّرْدَاءِ , عَنِ النَّبِيِّ صَلَّى اللَّهُ عَلَيْهِ وَسَلَّمَ , قَالَ : « خَلَقَ اللَّهُ آدَمَ حِينَ خَلَقَهُ , فَضَرَبَ كَتِفَهُ الْيُمْنَى , فَأَخْرَجَ ذُرِّيَّةً بَيْضَاءَ , كَأَنَّهُمُ الذَّرُّ , وَضَرَبَ كَتِفَهُ الْيُسْرَى , فَأَخْرَجَ ذُرِّيَّةً سَوْدَاءَ كَأَنَّهُمُ الْحُمَمُ , فَقَالَ لِلَّذِي فِي يَمِينِهِ : إِلَى الْجَنَّةِ وَلَا أُبَالِي , وَقَالَ لِلَّذِي فِي كَفِّهِ الْيُسْرَى : إِلَى النَّارِ وَلَا أُبَالِي ".

- ↝ You might ask yourself what the purpose is of saying "right shoulder" and "left shoulder". The reason for that is because according to Islam, the right shoulder represents the good deeds and the left shoulder which means the left-hand, represents the bad deeds. Therefore according to Muhammad, the white people represent the good deeds and the black people represent the bad deeds or the evil one, this is why Muhammad describes his god as someone who has two hands but both of them are right hands!
- ↝ Additional to that not only the white people are made from the right shoulder which means right hand, but even they would be placed on the right hand of Allah for they are the righteous according to Islam, while the black people would be on the left side.

The Prophet said: "Those who are just and rational will be with Allah, Most High, on thrones of light, at the right hand of the Most Merciful, those who are just in their rulings and in their dealings with their families and those of whom they are in charge." Muhammad said in his Hadith: "And both of His hands are right hands." Sunan an-Nasa'i 5379

FASTING AND SEX

During Ramadan it is forbidden for a Muslim to have sexual relationships with his wives at daytime as we read:

Permitted to you, on the night of the fasts, is the approach to your wives. They are your garments and ye are their garments. Allah knoweth what ye used to do secretly among yourselves; but He turned to you and forgave you; so now associate with them, and seek what Allah Hath ordained for you, and eat and drink, until the white thread of dawn appear to you distinct from its black thread; then complete your fast Till the night appears; but do not associate with your wives while ye are in retreat in the mosques. Those are Limits (set by) Allah: Approach not nigh thereto. Thus doth Allah make clear His Signs to men: that they may learn self-restraint. Q 2:187 Yusf Ali Translation.

In case you do not know, fasting according to Islam, is about forbidding any kind of food or liquid entering the mouth until the sunset, and then you can eat as much as you like, all night until the sunrise. However, we see that Muhammad used to kiss his wife doing the daytime and not only that, he sucks tongue!

"The Prophet used to kiss her and suck her tongue when he was fasting". Sunan Abi Dawud 2386

For sure there's nothing wrong with the man doing that with his wife, but the problem is, he told his followers while fasting not to approach the women during daytime, but yet he himself as usual was doing the opposite.

I inserted my finger in her vagina!

From one of the biggest Islamic scholars' websites Islamweb.net we quote the following question and answer:

The question:

In the month of Ramadan and after the dawn prayer, I did foreplay with my wife, and I inserted my finger inside her vagina! And nothing came out of it, and I did not cum too. Therefore what is the rule of Islam on fasting in that day, is fasting accepted or rejected?

The answer fatwa 66731: *We are thankful for Allah and Allah pray on the prophet and salute him that being said we would like to inform you that it is a requirement for the person who is fasting to stay away from any act deflate is fasting, and there's no question that foreplay with your wife is a huge risk and would deflate your fasting, as we mentioned before in fatwa(answer according to Islam) Number 113621, however if you did not have a orgasm your fasting it is still accurate, regarding your wife have fasting is not accepted because you inserted your finger inside her vagina and this is the opinion of many scholars.*

السؤال

في رمضان هذا العام وبعد صلاة الفجر، أخذت أداعب زوجتي، وأدخلت أصبعي في فرجها، ولكنه لم ينزل منها شيء، وكذلك لم ينزل مني شيء. فما حكم صيام هذا اليوم، هل صحيح أم إنه فسد ؟

الإجابة

الحمد لله والصلاة والسلام على رسول الله وعلى آله وصحبه، أما بعد:

فننبه أولا على أن الصائم يتعين عليه الابتعاد عما يفسد صيامه, ولاشك أن مداعبة الزوجة له خطر كبير على صحة الصيام كما سبق في الفتوى رقم: 113621.

وإذا لم يحصل منك إنزال للمني فصيامك صحيح.

وبالنسبة لزوجتك فقد بطل صيامها بناء على أن دخول شيء فى الفرج مبطل للصيام, وهو مذهب كثير من أهل العلم,

Unexplained behavior with children

I believe all of you know already, that Muhammad married a six years old child, a baby girl: *'Aisha said "that the Prophet married her when she was six years old and he had full intercourse with her when she was nine years old, and then she remained with him for nine years"* (i.e., till his death). Sahih al-Bukhari 5133

According to Islamic history books, Muhammad died at the age of 63. 'Aisha lived with him for 9 years, which means that at the time he married with 'Aisha the age of Mohammad was 63-9=54 years.

At this point we should ask ourselves a very simple question:

1. Why would a man of this age think for a second about having a sexual relationship with a child at the age of six.
2. Based on Muslims' defense they would say to you: he did not have sex with

her until she became nine years old.

3. The fact is she was his wife at the age of six, not at the age of nine, and between the age of six and nine, he used to fondle her, and when she completed the age of nine according to 'Aisha he had complete sexual intercourse with her.

Narrated 'Aisha: *The Prophet married to me when I was a girl of six. We went to Medina and stayed at the home of Bani-al-Harith bin Khazraj. Then I got ill and my hair fell down. Later on my hair grew again and my mother, Um Ruman, came to me while I was playing in a swing with some of my girlfriends. She called me, and I went to her, not knowing what she wanted to do to me. She grabbed me by the hand and made me stand at the door of the house. I was breathless then, and when my breathing became relaxed, she took some water and rubbed my face and head with it. Then she took me into the house. There in the house I saw some Ansari women who said, "Best wishes and Allah's Blessing and a good luck." Then she entrusted me to them and they prepared me (for the marriage). Unexpectedly Allah's Apostle came to me in the forenoon and my mother handed me over to him, and at that time I was a girl of nine years of age.* Sahih al-Bukhari 3894.

So according to this story Aisha was a wife at the age of six and she moved totally to her "husband's" house at the age of nine.

Narrated 'Aisha: *that the Prophet married her at the age of six years old and he had intercourse with her when she was nine years old, and then she remained with him for nine years (i.e., till his death).* Sahih al-Bukhari 5133.

But what happened between her age of 6 and 9? Why Muhammad married her at 6 if he will not have her? The fact is that till he had intercourse with her at the age of nine, he had been molesting her for all these years.

"When the two circumcised (clitoris of the woman and man part) parts meet, then bath is obligatory. The Messenger of Allah and I did that, and we bathed." Sunan Ibn Majah Vol. 1, Book 1, Hadith 608.

What 'Aisha is talking about here is Muhammad rubbing his private part against her private part, but yet no intercourse, for reason that at that age she was too young for sex.

This is why Muhammad made it lawful for Muslims to get married to children, this is why the word pedophile is not used in Islamic countries, for it is legal to be a pedophile actually Mohammad, the best man of Islam is giving the good example, so what about the rest?

This is why we are finding Qur'an 65:4 speaking of divorcing girls who did not have their menses yet because they are too young. *"And for those who have no courses meaning The same for the young, who have not reached the years of menstruation"* Tafsir bn Kathir.

And we find more strange and weird behavior, not only for little girls, but for boys too!

"Usama fell at the edge of the door and cut his face. The Messenger of Allah said: 'Remove the harm (the blood) from him,' but I was repulsed by that. He started to suck the blood and remove it from his face, then he said: 'If Usamah were a slave girl, I would have beautified him and dressed him until I married him off.'" Sunan Ibn Majah Vol. 3, Book 9, Hadith 1976.

1. This child is not even from his family.
2. I never heard of someone sucking the blood from the face of a person or a child because he fell down to the floor, that is possibly accepted if the story would have been about the child being bitten by a snake, but as we see the kid in the story just fell down!
3. To make the story more strange and weird, while he was sucking the blood of the child's face, Muhammad wished the boy would have been a girl, so he might dress her up with the most beautiful women's clothing!
4. I find such a wish very disturbing, especially for Arab men and their culture which considers the male gender as the best!
5. This strange behavior of Muhammad did not stay personal but yet he encourages his followers to also lust after children.

It is very obvious, that Muhammad always recommends sexual relationships with children, this story is an example of that:

Jabir said: "I married a woman and went to the Prophet, he said: 'O Jabir! Have you married?' I said: 'Yes.' He said: 'A virgin or a previously married?' I said: previously married.' He said: 'Why didn't you marry a young girl, so that you may play with her and she play with you?' I said: 'O Messenger of Allah! Abdullah (his father) died and left behind seven - or nine - daughter, so I have brought someone who can look after them." (He said:) *"So he supplicated for me."* Jami` at-Tirmidhi 1100.

Narrated Jabir bin `Abdullah: *My father died and left seven or nine girls and I married a matron. Allah's Messenger said to me, "O Jabir! Have you married?" I said, "Yes." He said, "A young virgin or a matron?" I replied, "A matron." he said, "Why not a young virgin, so that you might play with her and she with you, and you might have fun with her and she have fun with you." I said, " 'Abdullah (my father) died and left nine or seven girls, and I dislike to marry a girl like them (in their age), so I married a woman so that she may look after them." On that he said, "May Allah bless you,"* Sahih Muslim 715 f.

a. What kind of advice this man who claims to be a prophet of God, is giving his men?
b. This man is not complaining about his marriage, and he did not mention anything about it, so what was the business of Muhammad to ask him such a private question, if his wife is virgin or not.
c. Imagine you meet a friend, and he asks you: is your wife's private part sealed or not?
d. Additional to all of this, he starts questioning the reasons of the marriage, and is creating a pedophile desire and temptation in the head of this man!
e. A true prophet of God doesn't encourage people to divorce and doesn't seduce the husband to look for another female, yet in the case of Muhammad the story is different as usual.
f. And if you think about this advice, of finding a young child to marry, you will find nothing but what is inside Muhammad's mind, his own desire and that explains his desire to marry someone at the age of six, for he thinks this is the best of all choices!
g. And that will lead us to understand that his very first marriage with his first wife Khadija, who was at least 15-20 years older than him, was not a choice he liked. Just because she was rich and he used to work for her he accepted to marry her for the sake of the money, as an opportunity not out of sexual desire nor love.

We divorce children but we don't marry them!

There are endless numbers of articles trying to defend the sexual relationship between a 54 years old man, and a six years old child.

And those articles are filled with fabrications to the point even that Muhammad supposedly got married to his child wife when she was 21 years old, which means she would have married him three years after his death!

And this kind of fabricating is being exposed by the statement of his wife 'Aisha herself: *'Aisha reported that Allah's Messenger married her when she was six years old, and he had full sexual-intercourse when she was nine, and when he died she was eighteen years old.* Sahih Muslim 1422 d.

Rules always are made for a reason, so if Muslims do not have child wives then what is the need of a law to teach you how to divorce children?

Qur'an 65:4 Tafsir al-Jalalyn. *And as for those of your women who no longer expect to menstruate if you have any doubts about their waiting period their prescribed waiting period shall be three months and also for those who have not yet menstruated because of their young age their period shall also be three months*

واللائي) بهمزة وياء وبلا ياء في الموضعين (ينسن من المحيض) بمعنى الحيض (من نسائكم إن)
ارتبتم) شككتم في عدتهن (فعدتهن ثلاثة أشهر واللائي لم يحضن) لصغرهن فعدتهن ثلاثة أشهر

Tafsir Ibn Kathir volume 8. Page 136. *Allah the Glorious explains the waiting period of the woman in menopause. And that is the one whose menstruation has stopped due to her older age. Her `counting period is three months instead of the three monthly cycles for those women whom menstruate, which is based upon the Cow chapter. Look at 2:228 The same for the young, who have not reached the years of menstruation. Their ` counting period is three months alike those in the ceasing of menstruation. This is the meaning of His saying; "and for those who have no courses"*

from Ubay bin Ka`b who said, "O Allah's Messenger! When the verse in chapter of the Cow was revealed prescribing the `counting period of divorce, some people in Al-Madinah said, 'There are still some women whose ` counting period has not been mentioned in the Qur'an. There are the young, and the old whose menstruation is discontinued, and the pregnant.' Later on, this Ayah was revealed,

عن أبي بن كعب ، قال : قلت لرسول الله - صلى الله عليه وسلم - : إن ناسا من أهل المدينة لما أنزلت
هذه الآية التي في " البقرة " في عدة النساء قالوا : لقد بقي من عدة النساء عدد لم يذكرن في القرآن
: الصغار ، والكبار اللائي قد انقطع عنهن الحيض ، وذوات الحمل . قال : فأنزلت التي في النساء
(القصرى : (واللائي ينسن من المحيض من نسائكم إن ارتبتم فعدتهن ثلاثة أشهر واللائي لم يحضن

So the Muslims do their best to fabricate stories about the age of 'Aisha when she slept with Muhammad and the age of her at her marriage, hoping that you would never find out these verses in the Qur'an about divorcing children but yet the Muslims do not marry kids!

Muhammad's intercourse with a crazy woman

"it was narrated from Thabet Ibn 'Anas a she has a mental issue(crazy) she said

prophet of Allah I have a need for you(sexual needs), the prophet replied call the mother of etc. take location of your choice and I will fulfill your needs, so he went with her privately till she got what you wanted" Sahih Muslim 2326.

The Muslim's translation of the same hadith is far from the truth: *Anas reported that a woman had a partial derangement in her mind, so she said. Allah's Messenger, I want something from you. He said: Mother of so and so, see on which side of the road you would like (to stand and talk) so that I may do the needful for you. He stood aside with her on the roadside until she got what she needed.* Sahih Muslim 2326.

وحدثنا أبو بكر بن أبي شيبة حدثنا يزيد بن هارون عن حماد بن سلمة عن [ص: ٣١٨١ 2326 4293] ثابت عن أنس أن امرأة كان في عقلها شيء فقالت يا رسول الله إن لي إليك حاجة فقال يا فلان انظري أي السكك شئت حتى أقضي لك حاجتك فخلا معها في بعض الطرق حتى فرغت من حاجتها

Muhammad's hands on a woman's breast!

"Narrated by Imam Al-Bue'sari he said: A Women came to the prophet and she said to him wipe my face with your hand, and invoke Allah for my sake, therefore the prophet wiped her face and invoked Allah for her sake, then she said Messenger of Allah move your hands down, and the prophet moved his hand down at her breast, then she said prophet move your hand more down and spread it out" Book of Al Mana'qib volume 6. Page 471. By Ibn 'Hajer.

« كِتَابُ الْمَنَاقِب   المطالب العالية بزوائد المسانيد الثمانية لابن حجر ...
قَالَ أَبُو بَكْرٍ (ابن أبي شيبة) : ثَنَا عَفَّانُ ، ثَنَا عَبْدُ الْوَارِثِ ، ثَنَا حَنْظَلَةُ ، عَنْ أَنَسٍ ، قَالَ: إِنَّ امْرَأَةً } أَتَتِ النَّبِيَّ فَقَالَتْ: يَا رَسُولَ اللَّهِ ، امْسَحْ وَجْهِي ، وَادْعُ اللَّهَ لِي ، قَالَ: فَمَسَحَ وَجْهَهَا وَدَعَا اللَّهَ تَعَالَى لَهَا ، قَالَتْ: يَا رَسُولَ اللَّهِ، سَفِّلْ يَدَكَ
{ فَسَقَّلَ يَدَهُ عَلَى صَدْرِهَا ، فَقَالَتْ: يَا رَسُولَ اللَّهِ ، سَفِّلْ يَدَكَ فَأَبَى، وَبَاعَدَهَا
تحاف الخيرة المهرة للإمام البوصيري ج٦ ص 471 ط دار الوطن للنشر – الرياض ت: دار المشكاة بإشراف أبي تميم ياسر بن إبراهيم

I have no comment except that it is Mr. Man forbidden to touch any part of the skin of any foreign woman which is not his wife. But yet the prophet has no problem to touch the face of the woman or her breast under the excuse of blessing her, and the women is asking for more to move his hand down, how far down we don't know!

Necrophilia and prophet!

The coming story is about when the mother of Muhammad's cousin 'Ali died and 'Ali was crying over her death, Muhammad did something totally strange.

When Fatima Binte Asad, mother of 'Ali died. At the time of her burial, the Messenger Allah took off his shirt dressed Fatima (the dead women) in it. Then the Holy Prophet himself lay in that grave with her. And after they buried her, people questioned about the reason of doing so (lay in that grave with her).they said prophet of Allah you did something nobody did ever before! The Holy Prophet replied: I dressed her with shirt so she will wear clothing of heaven and I slept with her in her grave to dismantle the pressure of her grave, she was one of the best women for me" Majm'a Al-Zawa'ed hadith 15400/ Ma'refat Al-'Sahaba hadith 273 book of Kaniz Al-'Umal 37609.

Note this hadith has been reported by tens of Islamic books and it is totally authentic.

لَمَّا مَاتَتْ فَاطِمَةُ أُمُّ عَلِيٍّ خَلَعَ رَسُولُ اللهِ صَلَّى اللهِ عَلَيْهِ وَسَلَّمَ قَمِيصَهُ وَأَلْبَسَهَا إِيَّاهُ وَاضْطَجَعَ فِي قَبْرِهَا ، فَلَمَّا سَوَّى عَلَيْهَا التُّرَابَ ، قَالَ بَعْضُهُمْ : يَا رَسُولَ اللهِ ، رَأَيْنَاكَ صَنَعْتَ شَيْئًا لَمْ تَصْنَعْهُ بِأَحَدٍ ، قَالَ : إِنِّي أَلْبَسْتُهَا قَمِيصِي لِتَلْبِسَ مِنْ ثِيَابِ الْجَنَّةِ وَاضْطَجَعْتُ مَعَهَا فِي قَبْرِهَا لأُخَفِّفَ عَنْهَا مِنْ ضَغْطَةِ الْقَبْرِ ، إِنَّهَا كَانَتْ أَحْسَنَ خَلْقِ اللهِ صَنِيعًا إِلَيَّ بَعْدَ أَبِي طَالِبٍ

We are going to analyze the two excuses in this story:

- The Muslims refuse totally any explanation that is claiming that their prophet had sex with a dead woman.
- Me myself I have no problem to believe in that, however the problem is if he was not having sexual intercourse with her in her grave what is the logic of what he did?
- When a woman died the Arab would strip her naked and wrap her with a sheet.
  - He took off his shirt
  - He slept with her in the grave
- The excuse is forgiveness and mercy! Since when if a prophet of God dresses someone with his shirt that person's sin should be forgiven. And if Muhammad slept with someone in the grave, Allah would make the punishment of the grave nicer, or the pressure of the grave less!
- Specially this woman here is not even a Muslim woman?

So if the excuse to sleep with her and to dress her with his clothing was forgiveness, then based on the Qur'an this is a false excuse for the following reason:

- she refused to accept Islam during her lifetime, actually the Qur'an confirms that no matter what, even when Mohammed begs for it, Allah will not forgive those who transgress against him by refusing Islam: Qur'an 63:6: Doesn't matter whether you beg forgiveness for them or do not beg forgiveness for them; Allah will never forgive them; surely Allah does not guide the transgressing people.

↬ As you see in the story, Muhammad had a very short prayer not even begging for anything, so either the Muslims have to accept, that their prophet practiced things against his own god's teachings, and that would make him the same as those who transgress against "God", or is he not supposed to follow the orders of his god Allah?

↬ Or they have to accept that this man had a mental illness.

↬ However, we will be waiting for the Muslims answer maybe they can find one in the coming millennium.

Muhammad the rapist can't wait!

There are many idiots in the west that keep defending the crimes of Islam, as an example dr. James White said "Anyone that says ISIS (Islamic State) is Islam, he is a liar" and I challenged him many times to debate me about it but as usual he escaped the humiliation of the exposure of his ignorance.

I challenge anyone in the world to tell me one thing ISIS did and Muhammad did not do?

He was a rapist, a thief, killer, child molester, even his own son's wife couldn't escape his sexual madness.

In the coming story yet another clear example of the criminal mentality Muhammad used to have.

While the Prophet was having intercourse with Safiyah Abu Ayyub waited the night at his door. When he saw the Prophet in the morning he said "Allahu Akbar." He had a sword with him; he said to the Prophet, "O Messenger of God, this slave woman had just been penetrated, and you killed her father, her brother, and her uncles from her mother's side and her father side, her husband, and the rest of her tripe, therefore I was so worry she might harm you." The Prophet laughed and said "Good." History of Al Tabari Volume 39, Zad Al-ma'ad by ibn al Qayim page 291 Al-Waqidi page 708.

وبات أبو أيوب الأنصاري قريبا من قبته آخذا بقائم السيف حتى أصبح فلما خرج رسول الله صلى الله عليه وسلم بكرة فكبر أبو أيوب فقال ما لك يا أبا أيوب ؟ فقال يا رسول الله دخلت بهذه الجارية وكنت قد قتلت أباها وإخوتها وعمومتها وزوجها وعامة عشيرتها ، فخفت أن تغتالك . فضحك رسول الله صلى الله عليه وسلم وقال له معروفا

- There are tons of articles portraying Muhammad as a person of mercy, at the contrary the truth is very ugly and disgusting.
- This woman is still in the land of her tribe, her family has just now been slaughtered by Muhammad, their blood not yet dry on his sword.
- All of this was not enough to stop this cowardly man from raping this woman on the same day.
- One of his men felt how dangerous it was to rape and sleep with the woman of whom he killed every family member.
- So he waited outside guarding the criminal from the revenge of that woman.
- After all it's a happy morning for Muhammad. The Prophet laughed and said "Good".

The holy shirt of the prophet

"I dressed her with shirt so she will wear clothing of heaven and I slept with her in her grave to dismantle the pressure of her grave"

Maybe an average person trying to analyze the story would not find something additional to what we said already, but in fact there is a lot more. Muhammad claimed that there is something called "heaven clothing" and if you dress yourself in this kind of clothing you will become as the following:

- VIP for Allah.
- The clothing provides you with total protection from Allah's punishment.
- The clothing of the prophet is kind of bullet proof from the anger of his god.
- The god of Islam accepts connection and corruption, so if I have someone that is close to Allah then I don't have to worry about going to jail, what in this case would be Eternal Hell!
- Somehow Allah and his prophet remind me of the corrupt leaders in the west like Clinton, Obama, Sarkozy, and the Italian mafia.
- Specially Allah announced clearly that he created the whole universe for the sake of Muhammad:

"Jibra'il came to the Prophet of Allah and said that Allah says: I have not created anyone who is more noble to me than you. I have created the world and all that is therein so that they may know the rank that you possess. I would not have created the world if I had not created you"

You can find a long article made by Muslims about that on this site sunnah.org. Or search the net for this title 'If not for you (O Muhammad!) I would not have created creation.

Final conclusion of this entire story

1. Muhammad cannot be considered a stable person.
2. Regardless if you strip the woman for the sake of forgiveness or not.
3. The failure to defend Muhammad has one single reason, namely nobody can defend madness.

In fact there's many Islamic scholars that issued Fatwa's (scholars issuing guidelines according to the teachings of Muhammad), who made it clear that a husband having sex with his dead wife's corpse is something lawful.

You can search as an example for this title "Moroccan Cleric Abd Al-Bari Al-Zamzami: Husbands May Have Sex with Dead Wife's Corpse; Women May Use Carrots as Vibrators" And if you search about sex with dead wife you would find some other videos of Muslim scholars, explaining why that is lawful.

And sometimes Muslims go mad with their god's teachings as an example this Fatwa from the official Mufti of Saudi Arabia. "Top Saudi cleric denies issuing fatwa 'allowing husbands to EAT wives if they are hungry'" express.co.uk

SEXUAL COMMUNITY NOT A SOCIAL ONE

We will show you some examples, which would present to us the mentality of Muhammad and his community in which their number one focus is sex and sexual practices.

Dr. Muhammad the sex consultant

I can provide thousands of quotations about the sexual activities, showing the madness of these stories, however I am going to provide for you what is enough for the educational purpose of this book.

It's very normal for men and women during the marriage to face all kinds of private issues, however I will give you some examples of the stories reported to us by the Muslims themselves, which exposes a side of Muhammad's sexual private life which is approved by his followers:

From a book of Dala'el Al-Nubuah which means the proof of the prophethood hadith # 2494. *The messenger of Allah went out with 'Umar Ibn Al-khatab and the woman appeared and in front of him and she said: oh Messenger of Allah I am a Muslim in women from the forbidden women(it's forbidden for the Muslims to rape her for she is a Muslim), and I have a husband in my house who is the same as a woman(cannot have sex), the Prophet said: call for your husband.*

The husband came and the Prophet said to him: what about what your wife is saying oh slave of Allah?
The man he said I swear by your head my head(his penis) never go dry for her!
The wife she said: he can't even do it once a month!
The Prophet said: do you hate him?
She answered, yes.
The prophet answered saying get the closer with you heads together, and he prayed may Allah make you like each other.

أَنَّ رَسُولَ اللَّهِ صَلَّى اللَّهُ عَلَيْهِ وَسَلَّمَ خَرَجَ وَعُمَرُ بْنُ الْخَطَّابِ مَعَهُ فَعَرَضَتِ امْرَأَةٌ ، فَقَالَتْ : يَا رَسُولَ اللَّهِ ! إِنِّي امْرَأَةٌ مُسْلِمَةٌ مُحَرَّمَةٌ ، وَمَعِي زَوْجٌ لِي فِي بَيْتِي مِثْلُ الْمَرْأَةِ ، فَقَالَ لَهَا النَّبِيُّ صَلَّى اللَّهُ عَلَيْهِ وَسَلَّمَ : « ادْعِي زَوْجَكِ » ، فَدَعَتْهُ وَكَانَ خَرَّازًا ، فَقَالَ النَّبِيُّ صَلَّى اللَّهُ عَلَيْهِ وَسَلَّمَ : « مَا تَقُولُ امْرَأَتُكَ يَا عَبْدَ اللَّهِ ؟ » فَقَالَ الرَّجُلُ : وَالَّذِي أَكْرَمَكَ مَا جَفَّ رَأْسِي مِنْهَا ، فَقَالَتِ امْرَأَتُهُ : مَا مَرَّةً وَاحِدَةً فِي الشَّهْرِ ، فَقَالَ لَهَا النَّبِيُّ صَلَّى اللَّهُ عَلَيْهِ وَسَلَّمَ : « أَتُبْغِضِيهِ ؟ » قَالَتْ : نَعَمْ ، فَقَالَ النَّبِيُّ صَلَّى اللَّهُ عَلَيْهِ وَسَلَّمَ : « أَدْنِيَا رُءُوسَكُمَا » ، فَوَضَعَ جَبْهَتَهَا عَلَى جَبْهَةِ زَوْجِهَا ، ثُمَّ قَالَ : اللَّهُمَّ أَلِّفْ بَيْنَهُمَا وَحَبِّبْ أَحَدَهُمَا إِلَى صَاحِبِهِ ، "

- When somebody claims to be a prophet of God, what is his business with a woman if she is not having sexual intercourse with her husband?
- When she told him about her sexual needs, she was expecting Muhammad to do what?
- He would force the husband to take Viagra?
- And why he asked her to bring her husband, for further questioning?
- It sounds like the pink panther detective movie, investigating sexual organs' defect!
- And now after Muhammad prayed for them, is that supposed to mean that the husband would be able to have sexual intercourse with his wife?
- And what makes this whole story more funny: it is written in a book with the following title "the proofs of the prophet hood"
- But what has his story to do with any proof of anything?

Female genital mutilation

There's thousands of articles, trying to cover the disgusting mentality of the man-made cult, where only man is allowed to enjoy his sexual pleasure, and Muslims are terrified about their female family members that they might enjoy sex or seek it.

Many articles try to explain it by claiming that there is a health benefit, but the fact behind this circumcision there's only one truth which is to reduce or to kill the sexual desire for the female. From an official Islamic website, I would quote:

The wisdom behind circumcision

With regard to a man, he cannot be clean from urine unless he is circumcised, because drops of urine collect underneath the foreskin and he cannot be sure that they will not drip and make his clothes and body impure. Hence 'Abd-Allaah ibn 'Abbaas was very strict on the issue of circumcision. Imam Ahmad said: Ibn 'Abbaas was very strict on this matter, and it was narrated that there is no Hajj and no prayer for him, i.e., if a person is not circumcised his Hajj and prayer are not valid. Al-Mughni, 1/115

With regard to the wisdom behind the circumcision of women, it is to regulate their desire so it will be moderate.

Shaykh al-Islam Ibn Taymiyah (may Allaah have mercy on him) was asked about whether women should be circumcised or not. He replied:

Praise be to Allaah. Yes, they should be circumcised, i.e., the top of the piece of skin that looks like a rooster's comb should be cut. The Messenger of Allaah (S) said to the woman who did circumcisions: "Leave something sticking out and do not go to extremes in cutting. That makes her face look brighter and is more pleasing to her husband." That is because the purpose of circumcising a man is to make him clean from the impurity that may collect beneath the foreskin. But the purpose of circumcising women is to regulate their desire, because if a woman is not circumcised her desire will be strong. Hence the words "O son of an uncircumcised woman" are used as an insult, because the uncircumcised woman has stronger desire. Hence immoral actions are more common among the women of the Tatars and the Franks, that are not found among the Muslim women. If the circumcision is too severe, the desire is weakened altogether, which is unpleasing for men; but if it is cut without going to extremes in that, the purpose will be achieved, which is moderating desire. And Allaah knows best. Majmoo' al-Fataawa, 21/114 https://islamqa.info/en/9412.

- ✧ It is so clear from their answer how they explain their concern and the reasoning behind it.
- ✧ We should reduce the woman's desire, is the true reason behind this crime against women, which destroy thousands of articles made by Muslims over the internet, with the claim of health benefit being just a cover up for the crime against women.
- ✧ This is what we notice, that Muhammad keeps talking about the sexual benefit of the man with which Allah would provide him in heaven, he encourages men to go and fight the Roman, in order to kidnap and rape the blond women of the Roman.
- ✧ Muhammad never mentioned any kind of sexual pleasure that women would enjoy in his Paradise, and the reason for that he is the kind of person who belongs to the kind of men who believe women are sex toys, therefore the women themselves are made for the pleasure of the man and it is the right of the man to enjoy these women, and if women are not allowed to enjoy their sexuality even in the heaven in the cult of Islam, so what do you expect ,women on earth would be better off?

Her vagina is wet!

Um Salama said, "Um Sulaim said, 'O Allah's Messenger Allah does not refrain from saying the truth! Is it obligatory for a woman to take a bath after she gets wet dream discharge?' He said, 'Yes, if she notices the water (i.e. discharge).' therefore Um Salama(one of his wives) smiled and said, 'Does a woman get wet dream with discharge?' Allah's Apostle said. 'Then why does a child resemble (its mother)?" Sahih al-Bukhari 3328.

Her mother Umm Salamah said: "Umm Sulaim came to the Prophet and asked him about a woman who sees in her dream something like a man sees. He said: 'Yes, if she sees water (in vagina), let her take a bath.' I said (Muhammad wife): 'You have embarrassed the women. Do women experience wet dreams?' The Prophet said: 'May your hands be rubbed with dust, how else does her child resemble her?'" Sunan Ibn Majah Vol. 1, Book 1, Hadith 600.

This story would bring many questions:

- ✧ Remember we are talking about people who lived 1400 years ago, yet a Muslim woman is asking the prophet whether she should wash her vagina or not.
- ✧ The prophet the sex consultant and expert corrected his wife, confirming that women do have wicked dreams about having sex with men.

↦ Then he wanted to emphasize his knowledge by adding one more statement to the confirmation he gave about women having sexual dreams and discharge, so he said *"May your hands be rubbed with dust, how else does her child resemble her?"*

↦ Which is obviously a false statement, because the baby will not resemble her mother, due to any liquid in her private part.

↦ In case you did not understand what he meant by saying: "how else does her child resemble her?", he meant the baby would be a girl!

The word water means sperm, so according to Muhammad women have sperm:

"The Messenger of Allah said: 'The man's water is thick and white, and the woman's water is thin and yellow. Whichever of them comes first, the child will resemble (that parent).'" Sunan an-Nasa'i Vol. 1, Book 1, Hadith 200.

(A Jewish man said) I have come to ask you about the child. He (the Prophet) said: The water of man is white, and The water of woman yellow, and when they have sexual intercourse and the male's water cum first upon the female's water, it is the male child that is created by Allah's Decree, and when the water of the female cum first upon the water of the male, a female child is formed by the Decree of Allah. The Jew said: What you have said is true; verily you are an Apostle. He then returned and went away. The Messenger of Allah said: He asked me about such and such things of which I have had no knowledge till Allah gave me that. Sahih Muslim 315 a.

In the Muslim translations in order to cover the falsehood of their prophet they added in this story the following:

I have come to ask you about the child. He (the Holy Prophet) said: The reproductive substance of man is white and that of woman (i. e. ovum central portion) yellow, and when they have sexual intercourse and the male's substance (chromosomes and genes) prevails upon the female's substance (chromosomes and genes), it is the male child that is created by Allah's Decree, and when the substance of the female prevails upon the substance contributed by the male, a female child is formed by the Decree of Allah. The Jew said: What you have said is true; verily you are an Apostle. He then returned and went away. The Messenger of Allah said: He asked me about such and such things of which I have had no knowledge till Allah gave me that. https://sunnah.com/muslim/3/38.

It is so sad that the Muslims tried to cover up the truth about the falsehood of the prophet by fabricating false translations.

Remember Mohammed was speaking about the water of the man and the woman, which he described as the man's water *"The water of man is white"* which is obviously the sperm of the man and the water of the woman what he described as "and *The water of woman yellow"* not what they added between two brackets **(chromosomes and genes)** We just mentioned on the page before this one how this woman came to ask Muhammad about her wet dream: *"The Messenger of Allah said: 'The man's water is thick and white, and the woman's water is thin and yellow. Whichever of them comes first, the child will resemble (that parent).'"* Sunan an-Nasa'i Vol. 1, Book 1, Hadith 200

You can find how Muslims expose each other, I quote from this website https://islamqa.info/en/2458: *"The water of the man is thick and white, and the water of the woman is thin and yellow. Whichever of the two prevails or comes first decides which parent the child will resemble."* (Agreed upon. Sahih Muslim, 469)"

And if we use from the same site another hadith translated by Muslims, we will see how they got themselves busted:

It was narrated from Anas that: *Umm Sulaim asked the Messenger of Allah about a woman who sees in her dream something like that which a man sees. The Messenger of Allah said: "If she sees that and has a discharge, then let her perform a bath." Umm Salamah said: "O Messenger of Allah, does that really happen?" He said: "Yes, the water of the man is thick and white and the water of a woman is thin and yellow. Whichever of them comes first or predominates, the child will resemble (that parent)."* https://sunnah.com/urn/1306430

قَالَ أَسْمَعُ بِأُذُنَيَّ . قَالَ جِئْتُ أَسْأَلُكَ عَنِ الْوَلَدِ قَالَ « مَاءُ الرَّجُلِ أَبْيَضُ وَمَاءُ الْمَرْأَةِ أَصْفَرُ فَإِذَا اجْتَمَعَا فَعَلاَ «مَنِيُّ الرَّجُلِ مَنِيَّ الْمَرْأَةِ أَذْكَرَا بِإِذْنِ اللَّهِ وَإِذَا عَلاَ مَنِيُّ الْمَرْأَةِ مَنِيَّ الرَّجُلِ آنَثَا بِإِذْنِ اللَّهِ

This is the reason I always keep repeating don't ever trust a Muslim's translation.

Now we continue with dr. Mohamed I mean Prophet Muhammad the sex consultant.

Open Marriage Sexual Relationship

A man came to the Prophet and said: My wife does not prevent the hands of a man who touches her. the prophet said: Divorce her. He the man said: I am afraid I can't resist my desire, I may crave for her. He said: Then enjoy her. Sunan Abi Dawud 2049.

You would notice in this story, how very relaxed Muhammad is talking like someone who lives in the hippies' city of Santa Cruz, California in the 1960s.

- ᴥ The man had a problem, his wife is acting like a slut, Muhammad provided the first solution:
  - ᴥ Divorce her
  - ᴥ The man he said: I am afraid I am so attached to her.
- ᴥ The prophet provided the second solution:
  - ᴥ Then as long as this is the case just enjoy her, then share her with the other men that come to your house.
- ᴥ Nowadays they call this kind of thinking: open-minded.

Which I believe is something stupid and would never be existing unless you're a perverted man or woman.

- ᴥ But the unique about this story is, Muhammad being a prophet of Allah, yet he doesn't mind, sharing one's wife with other men is his best solution. And to have an open marriage sexual relationship, as it used to be before Islam. If you remember we mentioned Zawaj Al-Rah't where one woman could sleep with up to 10 men, until she became pregnant, and then she would choose the father.

And you would notice right away the teaching and the practice of Muhammad contradicts the teaching of the Bible 180°.

Proverbs 10:9 (KJV) ⁹ *He that walketh uprightly walketh surely: but he that perverteth his ways shall be known.*

Hebrews 13:4 (KJV) ⁴ *Marriage is honourable in all, and the bed undefiled: but whoremongers and adulterers God will judge*

Again we see Muhammad contradicting himself, because for example in different stories his judgement was very harsh when it's come to adultery, ordering people to be stoned for having illegal intercourse with one person or partner only. So how come in this case of the wife having multiple boyfriends, instead of calling for punishment Muhammad advised the man to enjoy her together with the rest.

And I think the reason for this is, in case the story is a private story(matter) which means the man spoke to Muhammad when he was alone, then he does not need to act and show how very conservative he is. So, if you would exist in the time of Muhammad, you'd better not consult him when he's alone, obviously he would encourage you to be wicked.

One night stand or three, it's fine

Previously we described for you the kind of sexual encounter called **Nika'h Al-Mut'a** and we explained to you the requirements for such a contract, which is nothing but the agreement between both male and female parties:

1. How much the male should pay the female for her service.
2. How long the duration.
3. And both then should pronounce certain words where the man would accept the conditions and the woman would accept the payments and the date.

An example of Muhammad's recommendation of how you will be able to have sexual intercourse with any woman you like by hiring her for sex would be: we read the following Hadith:

Allah's Messenger (Allah pray on him and salute him) said, "If a man and a woman agree to share the bed their time should last for three nights, and if they like to continue (their sexual practice), they can do so; and if they want to separate, they can do so." Sahih al-Bukhari 5119.

- ✤ Imagine if one of Christ's apostles said that a man and a woman can share the bed for sexual intercourse without marriage for three days and three nights and if you like to increase feel free!
- ✤ And yet the Muslims claim that Islam is a conservative religion!
- ✤ And you would notice that the same person, here promoting adultery said if a married woman commits adultery, she should be stoned!
- ✤ In other words in Islam you can engage in adultery as long as you practice it the way Muhammad likes it.

And the fact is that this kind of sexual contract is even mentioned in the Qur'an.

It is Forbidden to you are married woman, except what your right hand possesses. This Allah has written for you, and all other women besides these are permitted to you, so that you may seek them out with your wealth, seeking chastity and not fornication. So when you have contracted pleasure Nika'h with them, then give them their words. There is no sin on you for whatever you agree to after this. Indeed, Alah is Knowing, Wise. Qur'an, 4:24.

And from the interpretation of that verse of Muhammad's cousin

Ibn 'Abas said: "it is also said that this means: so that you buy with your money captives; and it is also said that this means: so that you should seek with your money Nik'ah to women for an agreed period of time (al-mut'ah) but the lawfulness of this practice was later abrogated"

One of the visible symptoms of Mohammed's brain disorder, namely most frequently contradicting himself, was the major reason for his Flip flap with the law and rules.

Allah's Messenger (Allah pray on him and salute him) he said: *O people, I had permitted you to contract sexual pleasure with women, but Allah has forbidden it now until the Day of Resurrection. So he who has any woman with this type of contract he should let her off, and do not take back the wages you offer them.* Sahih Muslim 1406 d.

And this is my challenge to the Muslims:

- As you claim that this is the story reported from the mouth of your prophet then where we can find the order of Allah that forbids this kind of intimate sexual encounter? Remember the Hadith said "**but Allah has forbidden it now until the Day of Resurrection.**"
- If the prophet has the authority to cancel the law of his own god, then did Muhammad or his god Allah found that he made a mistake by allowing such a practice so he wanted to fix that mistake?

But what make this crazier is that after he approved the three-night stand, then he forbade it then he allowed it, then he forbade it????

Narrated by Imam Ahmad from others, and narrated by Ibn Al Bir and Al-Shafi'I said: *as I know does nothing Allah made it forbidden and then he made it lawful and then made it forbidden except the sexual pleasure contract (Mut'a).* Book of Nika'h Al-Mu'gni volume 7, page 137.

حكاه الإمام أحمد عن قوم ، وذكره ابن عبد البر وقال الشافعي : لا أعلم شيئا أحله الله ثم حرمه ، ثم أحله ثم حرمه ، إلا المتعة . فحمل الأمر على ظاهره ، وأن النبي صلى الله عليه وسلم حرمها يوم خيبر ، ثم أحلها في حجة الوداع ثلاثة أيام ، ثم حرمها

It is so clear that the god of Muhammad is not sure! However, the opinion above is what the Sunni Muslims believe so what about the Shia?

Why Shi'at Muslims still keep on practicing Mut'a

There are many other references which prove us that there is something fishy about the reasons and about who might have been the one forbidding this practice, which made me believe that the Shi'at Muslims are on the right track, namely this practice never was forbidden by Muhammad or "Allah".

Narrated 'Imran bin Husain: *The Verse of Mut'a was revealed in Allah's Book, so we performed it with Allah's Apostle, and nothing was revealed in Qur'an to make it illegal, nor did the Prophet prohibit it till he died. But the man (Omar) just expressed what his own mind suggested.* Sahih Bukhari Volume 6, Book 60, Number 43. Sahih Muslim 1226 c. Sahih Muslim 1226 g, h.

From the narration about this story, which is authentic we would learn the following:

- Muhammad did practice the one or three nightstands sex contract himself.
- That Muslims in his time practiced it too.
- Never ever in the Qur'an we find any verse that forbade this practice.
- And **all** the Muslims practiced it until Muhammad's death.
- And based on other reports it was 'Umar the caliph who made such a practice to be forbidden.

Abu Nadra narrated: *While I was in the company of Jabir b. 'Abdullah, a person came to him and said that Ibn 'Abbas and Ibn Zubair differed on the two types of Mut'as (Mu'ta of Hajj and Mut'a of women), whereupon Jabir said: We used to do these two during the lifetime of Allah's Messenger Allah pray on him and salute him, but Umar then forbade us to do them, and so we did not revert to them.* Sahih Muslim 1405 e. Sahih Muslim 1249.

Jabir b. 'Abdullah reported: *We contracted temporary marriage giving a handful of palm date or flour as a payment during the lifetime of Allah's Messenger Allah pray on him and salute him and throughout the time of Abu Bakr until 'Umar forbade it in the case of 'Amru bin Huraith.* Sahih Muslim 1405 d.

This is why the Shi'at Muslims still keep on practicing the sexual intercourse contract, and as I said I totally agree with their point of view.

Even if she is on her camel saddle

The messenger of Allah said: 'Do not do that. If I were to command anyone to prostrate to anyone other than Allah, I would have commanded women to prostrate to their husbands. By the One in Whose Hand is the soul of Muhammad! No woman can fulfill her duty towards Allah until she fulfills her duty towards her husband. If he asks her sex even if she is on her camel saddle, she should not refuse." Sunan Ibn Majah Vol. 3, Book 9, Hadith 1853.

The previous statement of Muhammad is such clear proof about what Islam considers the duty of women in society.

- ✤ The man is the god, after God on earth.
- ✤ It's forbidden to worship any but God, but it is the wish of Muhammad to make the women worship the man.
- ✤ Plus a total obedience is very much required, the good woman considered the one who never says no to sex, even on the road on top of her camel!
- ✤ But for sure we will never find the statement affirming the opposite like: a man cannot refuse sleeping with his wives, in fact the Qur'an made very clear that a man indeed can do so:

Qur'an 4:128: *If a wife fears cruelty or desertion on her husband's part, there is no blame on them if they arrange an amicable settlement between themselves; and such settlement is best; even though men's souls are swayed by greed. But if ye do good and practice self-restraint, Allah is well-acquainted with all that ye do.* Ysuf Ali Translation.

May I remind you of the story about the second wife of Muhammad, when this woman became old Muhammad started thinking about getting rid of her, and he stopped showing any attraction or having sex with this woman. As usual he claimed that his god gave him the okay not to have sex with his wife as part of an agreement, whereupon this poor old woman made the young beautiful wife 'Aisha agree that if she convinced Muhammad not to divorce her, she ('Aisha) can have the day scheduled for him to visit her.

Narrated Ibn 'Abbas: *Sawdah feared that the Prophet was going to divorce her, so she said: 'Do not divorce me, but keep me and give my day to 'Aisha. Therefore he did so, and the following was revealed: Then there is no sin on them both if they make terms of reconciliation between themselves, and making settlement is better (4:128). So whatever they agree to make peace in something then it is permissible."* Jami` at-Tirmidhi Vol. 5, Book 44, Hadith 3040.

The wives of Muhammad used to fight over that day when he came to visit them, not because of missing him, but because of the gifts coming into the house he will be staying in that day. The fight over the gifts and the money was so obvious and clear as we read:

Narrated ʿUrwa from ʿAisha: *The spouses of Allah's Messenger were in two parties. One group consisted of ʿAisha, Hafsa, Safiya and Sauda; and the other group consisted of Um Salama and the other wives of Allah's Messenger. The Muslims knew that Allah's Messenger loved ʿAisha, so if any of them had a gift and wanted to give to Allah's Messenger he would delay it, till Allah Messenger had come to ʿAisha's home-based and then he would send his gift to Allah's Messenger in her home. The group of Um Salama chatted the matter together and decided that Um Salama must demand Allah's Messenger to tell the people to send their gifts to him in whatever wife's house he was. Um Salama told Allah's Messenger of what they had said, but he did not reply. Then those wives asked Um Salama about it. She said, "He did not say anything to me." They asked her to talk to him once again. She talked to him again when she met him on her day, but he gave no reply. When they asked her, she responded that he had given no reply. They said to her, "Talk to him till he gives you a answer." When it was her turn, she talked to him again. He then said to her, "Do not hurt me regarding Aisha, as the Divine Inspirations do not come to me on any women's clothing except that of Aisha." On that Um Salama said, "I regret to Allah for hurting you." Then the group of Um Salama called Fatima, the daughter of Allah's Messenger and sent her to Allah's Messenger to say to him, "Your wives demand to treat them and the daughter of Abu Bakr on equal terms." Then Fatima carried the message to him. The Prophet said, "O my daughter! Don't you love whom I love?" She replied agreeing and returned and told them of the situation. They requested her to go to him again but she refused. They then sent Zainab bint Jahsh who went to him and used harsh words saying, "Your wives appeal to you to treat them and the daughter of Ibn Abu Quhafa(ʿAisha) on equal terms." On that she raised her voice on ʿAisha so that Allah's Messenger looked at ʿAisha to see whether she would respond. ʿAisha started replying to Zainab till she silenced her. The Prophet then looked at ʿAisha and said, "She is really the daughter of Abu Bakr."* Sahih al-Bukhari 2581.

And this is one of many stories exposing the ways of Muhammad and how he didn't treat people who lived around him based on justice and being fair but based on his sexual desire. Where his favorite women in bed come first, and how justice is the last of his concerns. How he always thinks about himself first, as long as he likes a woman, then why should he care about the rest of his wives and their feelings, or about being fair, yet the Muslims have tens of thousands of articles speaking of the best of mankind Muhammad. Though clearly, he cannot even be fair and just within his own household, so imagine how he is with the strangers!

If I got horny what I should do as a Muslim?

Now we know that in Christianity you are encouraged to fight temptation, and temptation here is not sex, it's a sexual desire for a person that is unlawful for you.

Hebrews 13:4 (KJV) *⁴ Marriage is honourable in all, and the bed undefiled: but whoremongers and adulterers God will judge.*

Though, this is not the case at all in Islam, and who is better to take as the best example amongst the best of Muslims? For sure his name is Muhammad, so let's see what he did when he got horny by looking at a strange woman.

Chapter: Recommendation to the one who sees a woman and is attracted to her, to go to his wife or slave woman and have intercourse with her.

Jabir reported that Allah's Messenger saw a woman passing by, and so he came to his wife, Zainab, as she was tanning a leather and had sexual intercourse with her. He then went to his Companions and told them:

The woman approach and retires in the shape of a devil, so when one of you sees a woman, he should come to his wife, for that will repel what he feels in his heart. Sahih Muslim 1403 a. Al-Kafi V 5/ 11 495

If you look at the title of the chapter, you can tell right away how sexuality turned from something beautiful to something ugly, from something based on love and feeling, transformed into lust and wickedness.

And it is so obvious that Muhammad clearly broke one of the 10 commandments given to Moses: *"You shall not covet your neighbor's wife; and you shall not desire your neighbor's house, his field, his male servant, his female servant, his ox, his donkey, or anything that is your neighbor's."* "Deuteronomy 5:21.

If you don't have intercourse the prophet will hate you

The focus in the teaching of Jesus lies clearly on serving the good, God and self-sacrifice, including staying away from temptation. But even compared to marriage, though considered lawful and nothing wrong with that, the one who chooses to serve God and community is considered higher in rank because of the self-sacrifice he chooses, as written in:

Matthew 19:

[10] His disciples say unto him, If the case of the man be so with his wife, it is not good to marry.
[11] But he said unto them, All men cannot receive this saying, save they to whom it is given.
[12] For there are some eunuchs, which were so born from their mother's womb: and there are some eunuchs, which were made eunuchs of men: and there be eunuchs, which have made themselves eunuchs for the kingdom of heaven's sake. He that is able to receive it, let him receive it.

Islam on the contrary teaches totally the opposite to the point that a person praying all night and fasting all day is a very bad person and obviously not a true Muslim, because he is not having intercourse whereas Muhammad confirms that this is the true way of Islam.

The wife of 'Uthman came and she said: O Messenger of Allah 'Uthman is fasting all day long and the praying all night long, therefore the prophet he went out and he was so angry carrying his shoe(with his hands) and he came to 'Uthman where you found him praying and he said: "Allah never sent me to be a monk but he sent me to be Hanif(a name of the group claimed to be the follower of Abraham), I fast and I pray and I do have intercourse with my Women so who ever except my lifestyle he should follow the same, and my lifestyle is F***ing(intercourse) women. Al-Kafi V 5/ 11 496 – Wasil Al-Shi'a 25157.

(قال : جاءت امرأة عثمان بن مظعون إلى النبي (صلى الله عليه وآله)
فقالت : يا رسول الله ، انّ عثمان يصوم النهار ويقوم الليل ، فخرج رسول الله (صلى الله عليه وآله)
مغضبا يحمل نعليه حتى جاء إلى عثمان فوجده يصلي فانصرف عثمان حين رأى رسول الله (صلى
الله عليه وآله) ، فقال له : يا عثمان ، لم يرسلني الله بالرهبانيّة ، ولكن بعثني بالحنيفية السمحة ، أصوم
واصلي وألمس أهلي ، فمن أحب فطرتي فليستن بسنتي ، ومن سنتي النكاح

It was narrated from Aishah that: the Messenger of Allah said: "intercourse is my way of life, and whoever does not follow my way of life he has nothing to do with me. Get married, for I will boast of your great numbers before the nations. Whoever has the means, let him get married, and whoever does not, then he should fast for it will diminish his desire." Vol. 3, Book 9, Hadith 1846.

The concern of Muhammad when it's come to others having a sexual relationship or not, can be explained as the following:

1. When Muhammad found out that 'Uthman is fasting all day and praying all night, I don't think he was upset that much to the point to make him a run with naked feet carrying his shoes just because a guy is so busy and being occupied with the worship of Allah, but he was afraid that the people would notice that he is the one who claims to be the prophet but yet he does not practice neither fasting all day nor praying all night. Therefore he just decided to stop 'Uthman from such a practice which is going to make him look like a hypocrite because the followers are praying and fasting and worshiping while he is focusing on sex and more women.
2. The second issue we notice is, that he is encouraging the Muhammadans to get married and have sexual intercourse to increase the number of Muslims, this is why increasing the number of Muslims is not a choice for Muslims, but it is about to become an obedience following the plan and the agenda of Muhammad.

And for sure we will not forget that even the Qur'an confirms the rejection of religious practices like spending one's life in devotion and chastity.

Dr. Muhammad Ghali's translation: Qur'an 57:27. *Thereafter We made to supervene on their tracks Our Messengers; and We made to supervene (after that) Isa son of Maryam, (1Jesus son of Mary) and We brought him the Injil; (The Book revealed to) and We made in the hearts of the ones who closely followed him compassion and mercy. And monasticism they innovated for themselves; in no way did We prescribe it for them, except for seeking the all-blessed Satisfaction of Allah; yet in no way did they pay heed to it as it should be truly heeded. So We brought the ones of them who believed their reward; and many of them are immoral.*

And again, remember I am using the Islamic translation, to avoid any accusations of Muslims, not because I agree with it.

The first Muslim nun's request was denied

You might be wondering what this title is about? The very moment we say the word nun, the Catholics come to our mind. Living in chastity has in fact nothing to do with the Catholics it is practiced by many other churches.

I am sure you heard some people claim that the Catholics are the founders of Islam, which I find a very stupid, ignorant statement because nobody fought the savage invasion of the Muslims as much as the Catholics. Because sexuality (is) one of the major and fundamental ingredients of Islam, and any kind of monkhood is totally rejected. The coming story is about a woman who requested to be a nun or to live in a monastic order or life and right away she was denied and forbidden from doing so:

Book of Al-kafi volume 5, page 509. *It was reported by the Imam Muhammad ibn Al-Ba'qer peace up on him that the women she came to him requesting the acknowledgment and approval of living monastic order or life, he said(the imam) and what chastity is for you?*

She said: it is not to get married.

He said and what for?

She said to get closer to Allah and for his blessing.

He said get out if there is a blessing for that Fatima peace up on her she have more right to get the blessing then you and no one can overcome her good deeds.

ما ورد عن الإمام محمد الباقر عليه السلام أنَّ امرأة قالت له: أصلحك الله إني امرأة متبتلة، فقال عليه السلام: «وما التبتل عندك»؟، قالت: «لا أتزوج»، قال عليه السلام:«ولمَ" ؟ قالت: «ألتمس بذلك الفضل»، فقال عليه السلام: «انصرفي، فلو كان في ذلك فضل، لكانت فاطمة عليه السلام أحقَّ به منك، إنه ليس أحد يسبقها إلى الفضل"

If there is no Eve neither Jews, no evil exist

One of the reasons I don't trust Muslims teaching me about their religion is the endless lies they come with and now I will give you an example, I will quote a few lines from an Islamic article:

*"Blame it on Eve! Eve in the Bible vs Quran. Just a quick study of the way the Bible treats Eve would explain the reason behind all the **problems** that the women are suffering today."*

I am not going to discuss the falsehood of the claim for now, because it is not really the purpose of this book, but the question is why they don't tell us the truth about what they believe that women are always the evil ones in Islam in fact Muhammad said in clear words that she is the devil himself:

Jabir reported that Allah's Messenger saw a woman, and so he came to his wife, Zainab, as she was tanning a leather and had sexual intercourse with her. He then went to his Friends and told them: The woman advances and retires in the shape of a devil, so when one of you sees a woman, he should come to his wife, for that will repel what he feels in his heart. Sahih Muslim 1403 a

- As you see with me, the prophet of the Muhammadans was looking at the body of a woman walking by so he got so horny, he followed his desire and he went to his wife leaving his friends waiting for him in his house, in order to satisfy his desire for the woman who had been walking by!
- But yet he blamed the woman who did nothing except walking in the street.
- And not only that he claimed that the woman is the devil himself!
- And I wonder if the woman is supposedly the devil himself and she comes in the image of a devil and she leaves in the image of the devil, then why Muhammad according to the Islamic belief had 13 women which makes 13 devils!

If you read the following statement from the mouth of Muhammad or Qathem which is his real name, saying:

Narrated Abu Huraira: The Prophet said, "But for the Israelis, meat would not decay and but for Eve, wives would never betray their husbands." Sahih al-Bukhari 3330 / 3399

Can we make it clearer than this? The woman is the devil and she is the reason for the sin of Adam to the point Muhammad claimed that she betrayed her husband Adam, not only that she committed sin.

The god of Islam told Muhammad that women are the majority of hellfire.

Women are the fuel of hellfire!

Women are the fuel of hellfire, but if you pay me you would not!

In the coming story we will see a scamming method used from the ancient days until now. For example, you might see some religious programs on TV, and though claiming to be Christians they in fact are businessmen and their job is to make you send them money by giving you the very scary news that you would end up in hellfire, however if you make a donation right now you can be saved(!) and this is exactly what Muhammad did practice 1400 years ago.

He (Muhammad) then walked on till he came to the women and addressed them and admonished them, and asked them to give alms, for most of them are the fuel for Hell fire. A woman having a dark cheek stood up and said: Why is it so, Messenger of Allah? He said: because you complain often and demonstration ungratefulness to your husband. And then they began to give alms out of their ornaments such as their earrings and rings which they threw on to the cloth of Bilal. Sahih Muslim 885 b.

Think about what we just heard, imagine someone is coming to you and saying: your kind as a female will be the fuel of the hellfire, and then he explained why, but before he explains he demands you to give him money and he is calling it "charity"

The reasons to go to hell for women are :

1. Often complaining
2. Demonstrating ungratefulness to their husbands.

So if these are the reasons to go to hell, how can someone justify the method: pay and you will be Okay? To make it simple, if someone would go to hell because he's a killer, then the solution should be, stop killing and repent.

If someone is committing adultery the solution should be, stop committing adultery and repent. But as you see Muhammad is giving them a somewhat different solution, if you pay me you will be okay, and you can keep your behavior and your attitude!!! Now I understand why people do say: "money talk", or "no money no honey", therefore if you'd like to enjoy the honey of my Paradise, then dig into your pocket, in this case Muhammad stripped those women from their jewelry.

Her menses and intellect the reason to go to hell!

I heard Muhammad making many mad statements, but the coming one not only I find it not logical, but it is literally stupid.

Once Allah's Messenger (Allah pray on him and salute him) went out to offer the prayer of holiday of Adha(blood sacrifice) or Al-Fitr(breakfasting) prayer. Then he passed by the women and said, "O Women! give charities, as I have seen that the majority of the inhabitants of Hell-fire were women." The Women questioned, "Why is it so, Allah's Messenger (Allah pray on him and salute him) ?" He replied, "You curse often and are ungrateful to your husbands. I have not seen anyone more deficient in intelligence and faith more than you. A vigilant reasonable man could be led astray by some of you." The women asked, "O Allah's Messenger (Allah pray on him and salute him)! What is deficient in our intelligence and religion?" He said, Is not the evidence of two women equal to the witness of one man? The women replied agreeing. He said, "This is the deficiency in her intelligence. Isn't it true that a woman can neither pray nor fast during her menses? The women replied agreeing. He said, "This is the deficiency in her religion." Sahih al-Bukhari 304.

The story in this account included more reasons to go to hell for women, in the previous report Muhammad counted two reasons for women to go to hell but this one has two additional reasons.

1. Women suffer from deficiency of intellect and intelligence! In other words, women are stupid therefore should go to hell!!
2. The other reason is that women have their menses, and that would add one more deficiency which is going to affect their faith. The reward for sure will not be the same as the man, because Islam forbids them from praying or fasting during the menses time!

⤣ I'm not going to talk much about how absolutely stupid and absurd this is, but it is clear evidence of discrimination.

⤣ Muslim women are not qualified to be a witness in the court of law just because of their sex or gender?

The female gender, according to the god of Islam has a deficiency to be capable of being a witness in the court of law, therefore women are only allowed to be witnesses if they are preapproved, and only in cases of borrowing money, as the Qur'an said, and in cases of giving birth or the death of an infant throughout delivery, because only females are allowed to be in the room.

WORDS FROM THE AUTHOR

I pray Muslims will read my words carefully. The objective of the book is to help Christians and Muslims or whoever is searching for the truthfulness of God. I end my book with my favorite verse in the bible;

"And ye shall know the truth, and the truth shall make you free." John 8:32

May The Lord bless us all.

Don't forget to get your copy of ALLAH & SEX Volume II

The author: Christian Prince. ©

To contact https://www.patreon.com/ChristianPrince
www.facebook.com/TheChristianprince/
https://www.minds.com/ChristianPrince

LIST OF REFERENCES

Volume I: Volume II: page number.

Abu Ash-Shaykh Al-Asbahaani   **II**: 56

Abu Baker   **I**: 50, 61, 73   **II**: 6, 39, 88, 102, 105, 106

Abu Dawud   **II**: 34

Abd Al-Bari Al-Zamzami   **I**: 86

Ahmad   **II**: 52

Al-Adab Al-Mufrad   **I**: 58

Al-Asrar Al-Fa'temeah, book of   **I**: 71

Al-'Athamah   **II**: 56

Al-Baihaqi   **II**: 60

Al-Ba'eth, book of   **II**: 103

Al Bidaya Wal Nihaya   **I**: 53, 54   **II**: 43, 101, 110, 118, 119, 123

Al-Bujaerymi   **II**: 132

Al-Faiq   **II**: 36

Assad Al-Gabah, book of   **II**: 144

Al-'Hawi   **II**: 41, 124

Al-Iste'ab hamesh, book of   **II**: 110

al-islamorg   **I**: 7   **II**: 94, 95, 135

Al-Jam' Al-Sageer   **I**: 57

Al-Kamel for Ibn Al-Athir   **I**: 20

Al-Kafi, book of   **I**: 71, 98, 99, 101, 104 **II**: 11, 18, 19, 21, 22, 24, 26

Al-Kashaf, book of   **II**: 41

Al Khasa's Al-Kubra   **I**: 39, 40

Al Magani, book of   **II**: 50, 51

Al-Ma'thalib, book of   **I**: 21, 22

Al Magazi wal Al-Saeer   **I**: 38

Al Mana'qib   **I**: 82   **II**: 71

Al-Mu'anaf   **I**: 35

Al-Mughni   **I**: 88

Al-Mu'harer book of   **II**: 45

Al-Nihaya   **II**: 36

Al Nisa'   **II**: 96, 97

Al-Qurtbi   **I**: 52   **II**: 131, 132

Al-Razi   **I**: 50, 51, 52

Al Sam'any   **II**: 82

Al-Shifa bta'reef   **I**: 42, 43, 44

Al Siarah Al- 'Halabia   **I**: 55

Al-Sunan Al-Kubra   **II**: 96, 97

Al 'Tabaqat Al-Kubra   **I**: 39

Al 'Tabari   **I**: 60, 84   **II**: 56

Al Tabrai   **I**: 59

altafsir.com   **I**: 72   **II**: 134

Al Tafsir Al-Kaber   **I**: 73

Al-Tanwir fi Sharih Al-jami' Al-'Saqir **I**: 1   **II**: 3

Al-Tirmidhi   **II**: 57

Al-Wahidi   **I**: 29,30

Al-Waqidi   **I**: 84   **II**: 90

Al-Zamakhshari   **II**: 56

americanpregnancy.org   **I**: 77

Assad Al-Gabah, book of   **II**: 111

Asbab Al-Nuzul, book of   **I**: 30, 53 **III**: 90

Ayatollah Ruhollah Khomeini   **II**: 87

Bada' Al-Fawa'ed   **II**: 25

Bidayat al-Mujtahid   **II**: 36

Bihar Al-Anwar, book of   **I**: 71   **II**: 67, 68, 78, 80

Book Al-Fawa'ed   **II**: 105, 106

Book Bida'e Al-Fawa'ed   **II**: 27, 28,

Bulugh al-Maram   **II**: 34, 39

(cms)ibn-jebreen.com   **II**: 65

Dala'el Al-Nubuah   **I**: 87

express.co.uk   **I**: 86

Fan Al-Nik'ah, book of   **II**: 11,

Fatawa Razaviyya   **II**: 22

Fat'eh Al-bari   **I**: 1   **II**: 3, 36, 112

Fateh Al-Bukhari, book of   **II**: 70

Fatwa   **I**: 77, 80, 89   **II**: 52, 53, 65, 66

Fiqih Al Mazaheb Al-Arba'a   **II**: 34

Hashiat Al-Jumal book of   **II**: 57

History of Islam, the   **I**: 20

https: //islamqa.info   **I**: 66, 88, 91   **II**: 52

http: //quranx.com   **II**: 75

https: //sunnah.com   **I**: 90, 91

Ibn 'Abbas   **I**: 20, 50, 52, 57, 94,96   **II**: 4, 6, 24, 25, 35, 39, 40, 42, 46, 47, 48, 56, 57, 69, 75, 85, 95, 96, 122, 134, 137

Ibn Abi Al-Dunia   **II**: 133

Ibn Al-Athir   **II**: 36

Ibn Al-Qaim   **I**: 84   **II**: 25, 53

Ibn 'Hajer   **I**: 1, 82

Ibn Hisham   **I**: 59

Ibn Ishaq   **I**: 59

Ibn Jarir Al-Tabari   **II**: 57

Ibn Kathir   **I**: 53, 54   **II**: 24, 25, 43, 61, 75, 93, 94, 118, 119130, 134, 136

Ibn Khuzaimah   **II**: 34

Ibn Mandoor   **II**: 36

Ibn Rushd   **II**: 36

Imam Abu-Baker Al-Shafi'e   **II**: 105, 106

Imam Abu Dawood   **I**: 25

Imam al-Bukhaari   **I**: 25   **II**: 76

Imam al-Nasaa'i   **I**: 25

Imam Al-Nawawi   **II**: 25, 29, 30

Imam Al-Siu'ti   **I**: 39, 40   **II**: 124

Printed in Poland
by Amazon Fulfillment
Poland Sp. z o.o., Wrocław

65642966R00067